"I am impressed by Angela's approach to this delicate subject. She has a solid grasp of the many different aspects to be considered and discussed with owners who need support when losing their companion."

— DR. SHANNON GAFFANEY, BVetMed, member of the
Royal College of Veterinary Surgeons (MRCVS)

"In her beautiful book, *When It's Time to Say Goodbye: Preparing for the Transition of Your Beloved Pet*, Angela Garner gives a very comprehensive and thorough guide to pet loss. She gently and caringly holds the reader's hand through all the difficult aspects while offering simple and practical advice. Angela's holistic approach focuses on the well-being of both people and their pets prior to bereavement, and she offers a unique understanding of how grief affects us and how to cope with the distress it brings. She validates pet loss and treats it with the same significance as the loss of a human loved one. I will definitely recommend this book to any of my clients who face the loss of their pet."

— DEIRDRE CHITWOOD, Tellington TTouch practitioner for
companion animals, Level 2 (Guild certified)

"Most pet owners know how painful it is to lose a much-loved animal companion, and I am pleased that all those who suffer this unique loss can now benefit from the compassion and support that runs throughout *When It's Time to Say Goodbye: Preparing for the Transition of Your Beloved Pet* by Angela Garner. Every aspect of loss is touched on, all with Angela's special blend of understanding, practicality, and empathy. I recommend it for all pet owners to help them through the inevitable sad loss of their beloved pet."

— MELINDA HILL, founder and project manager of Environmental
Animal Sanctuary and Education (EASE)

"Humans are meant to outlive their pets, but what do we do when the death of our companion looms? Angela Garner's advice on how to support ourselves, our children, and other family pets through the grieving process is wise and compassionate."

er dog trainer,
Alpha Project

"A conversation about our pets passing on is uncomfortable for most of us. It is one we tend to avoid even the thought of until the time might be upon us. *When It's Time to Say Goodbye* empowers and guides people at a very emotional time, before and after an animal has passed. Saving the guardian unnecessary toil and emotional trauma, the information and activities in this book prepare and steer you step by step with sensitivity. Long overdue, this guide will be an immense help and support for many at a difficult time. A MUST read for every pet owner."

— DIANE BUDD, animal communicator, healer, and author of
Energy Medicine for Animals: The Bioenergetics of Animal Healing

WHEN IT'S TIME TO SAY GOODBYE

Preparing for the Transition of Your Beloved Pet

ANGELA GARNER

FINDHORN PRESS

Findhorn Press
One Park Street
Rochester, Vermont 05767
www.findhornpress.com

Text stock is SFI certified

Findhorn Press is a division of Inner Traditions International

Disclaimer

The information in this book is given in good faith and is neither intended to diagnose
any physical or mental condition nor to serve as a substitute for informed medical
advice or care. Please contact your health professional for medical advice and treatment.
Neither author nor publisher can be held liable by any person for any loss or damage
whatsoever which may arise from the use of this book or any of the information therein.

Cataloging-in-Publication Data for this title is available from the Library of Congress

ISBN 978-1-64411-121-5 (print)
ISBN 978-1-64411-122-2 (ebook)

Printed and bound in the United States by Lake Book Manufacturing, Inc.
The text stock is SFI certified. The Sustainable Forestry Initiative® program promotes
sustainable forest management.

10 9 8 7 6 5 4 3 2 1

Edited by Nicky Leach
Illustrations by Angela Garner
Text design and layout by Damian Keenan
This book was typeset in Calluna, Calluna Sans,
with Hermann used as a display typeface

To send correspondence to the author of this book, mail a first-class letter to the
author c/o Inner Traditions • Bear & Company, One Park Street, Rochester,
VT05767, USA, and we will forward the communication, or contact the author directly
at **www.petlosspress.com.**

This book is dedicated to the memory of

my dear mother, Eva May,

who died too young to see her three daughters grow up.

She will always be remembered with love.

Contents

FOREWORD

I am delighted to write the foreword to this very special book, both as a veterinarian and as an owner who has experienced the challenges of pet bereavement.

The loss of an animal, regardless of the attachment, is something we have to deal with as veterinary surgeons on a regular basis. Most vets have a practical approach to death: some become emotionally detached, some wear their hearts on their sleeves, but all of us will be affected at some level.

Supporting owners through these sometimes difficult times can be equally daunting. Many of us will never have received bereavement counselling as undergraduate students, although fortunately that has changed within the veterinary school curriculum of today. However, it can be challenging to really "understand" bereavement until we are forced to the other side of the consulting table. Unfortunately, the loss of an animal, whether from euthanasia, illness, or accident, is both inevitable and harrowing for all involved.

When I said goodbye to my constant companion for 12 years (my faithful running partner, on-call late-night protection unit, giver of unconditional love and keeper of secrets), I finally understood the term "heartbroken". His name was Frisby, and to me he was the best dog in the world. When I had to say goodbye for the first time as an owner rather than as a vet, as a client rather than employee, as a distraught mum rather than detached professional, I did so from the other side of the consulting table. Frisby left this world with his head on my knee in the sunshine, surrounded by people who loved him. From the other side of the consulting table I was proud to be a vet.

Death leaves a heartache no one can heal;
love leaves a memory no one can steal.
— Anon

In her book, Angela embraces some difficult areas that are often not spoken about but will be familiar to many. The section on how to help children through pet bereavement is particularly poignant. This book is a vital companion to anyone who cares for or works with animals and provides an armoury of skills to guide and support you through testing times. There are a number of activities to help people through specific areas of difficulty, and this book will be indispensable to those who find themselves facing loss—before, during, and after bereavement.

The contents are based on Angela's own professional experience as a pet bereavement specialist, and have been developed over years of supporting people through loss, with the addition of very personal stories where appropriate.

Victoria M. Nicholls, veterinary surgeon, BSc (Hons), BVetMed, Cert AVP (EM), Cert AVP (ED), BAEDT, MRCVS

What This Book Is About, and Who It Is For

As I begin to write this book, my heart feels heavy, not for myself but for a dear friend who today faces the loss of her beautiful golden retriever. She is a wonderful advocate of all animals, and because she cares she is offering her beloved canine friend one final act of kindness—to have him "put to sleep" before he starts to suffer.

At over 15 years old, he's reached a grand age for a retriever. He has been with my friend through the shock and grief of the sudden and unexpected loss of her husband, offering companionship and warmth during dark and lonely times. I look at my little dog lying beside me as I write, and hope, like all other loving canine guardians, that we have a good few years together ahead of us. But I know that one day it will most likely be me who needs to find the courage to make one of the hardest decisions that guardians of companion animals face.

Maybe you are in a similar situation to my friend, or perhaps you have already lost a beloved pet. If so, this book is for you. Whether the loss is recent, or even some time ago, this book will gently help to guide you through the process of grief from the loss of a cherished pet. Together, we'll look at what it means to love and ultimately lose a pet, how to work through it, and importantly, how to come out the other side to reconnect with your own life. There is no way around the grief; we can't avoid it. We grieve because we care, and we need to find our way through the many twists and turns that our individual journey creates. This book is written so that you don't have to go through the process alone. That's important, because grief itself can bring a significant sense of loneliness, even when surrounded by other people, perhaps making you feel as though no one truly understands.

Together, we'll approach the fears and concerns that so often arise leading up to the death of a pet. We'll look at ways to face the worries and unknown factors of anticipated pet loss to help you to understand what is happening and what can be done, and to work out the best way forward. The idea is to leave "no stone unturned" so that all the knotty areas concerning the death of a beloved animal have at least some coverage.

This book offers support—not with a multitude of placatory messages but to say it as it is: it's okay to feel what you feel, whatever that may be, to reassure you that although the grief at times may seem insurmountable you can, and will, get through it.

The intention of this book is to help you recognize and remember the essence of your pet's life. To value the love you had for them and the loyalty and affection you received in return—most special gifts. To understand that such love is never wasted, and what you had together meant something: it was real, remains real, and will do so for a very long time.

Finally, know that there is hope beyond the pain and distress you may be feeling. Your beloved companion animal will always be part of your life—just now in a different way, held within the warm and priceless memories echoing through the times you shared.

How the Book Works

People often say "time is a great healer", but this does not really help you cope when you are deep inside the raw grief that pet loss can bring. This book contains activities that will gently guide you through the different "seasons" of grief, with simple suggestions and ideas to help you approach and work through each part of the process.

You can read through the book from beginning to end or dip in and out as needed. Initially, you may need the Preparing for Pet Loss section, or maybe you've already been bereaved so feel drawn to the 'Coping with Grief' section. Take whichever parts work for you at the time, and maybe visit other sections later on, if and when they become more relevant to your particular grief journey.

Different activities are offered throughout the book, and again, I advise that you work with those to which you are drawn. There's no pressure to do anything other than what feels right for you, which, of course, only you will know.

When looking at end-of-life issues it is important to look at all aspects, including the practicalities, particularly when preparing for the loss of a much-loved companion animal. So you will find that I address such things in detail in some areas. Anything that isn't relevant to your particular situation can be ignored. You may notice in the Preparing for Pet Loss section that there is a strong emphasis on the welfare of the animals as well as support for the people who care for them. The practical sections aren't "fluffy"; they are designed to get right to the point, address current needs, and make things clearer during what is potentially a confusing time.

We can't talk about pet bereavement without thinking about the human–animal relationship. Anyone who has ever cared for and loved an animal, however large or small, will know that a deep and significant connection or bond can develop. This can apply to working and service animals, too.

As a testament to this, I'll mention a documentary I saw years ago about the American soldiers who, on returning home from the long conflict in Vietnam, had to leave their beloved canine partners behind. The intensity of working in that war zone had caused such a deep and abiding bond with their dogs, whose senses and heightened awareness had saved their lives on many occasions, they still mourned these brave canines more than 20 years later. Personally, I feel that the special relationship we have with other species needs to be honoured and celebrated, and it is because we care and love that we feel their loss so keenly.

Finally, you'll notice that I use the word "guardian" rather than "owner" in an attempt to find a more fitting description for the role of caring and protecting beloved companion animals. "Pet carer" or "pet parent" are other options, but to be consistent we will stay with "guardian".

PART ONE

· · · · · · ·

Preparing for Pet Loss

1

Preparing Your Heart
and Mind for Loss

My own experience of caring for an elderly dog is that I find myself watching him more closely, and there is an underlying anxiety that was not there before. "Why hasn't he finished his breakfast?" I hear myself saying to my husband, as our little dog has always had such a good appetite. Or "Is he limping? Does he need more joint supplements?" Any small issues are promptly checked by the vet.

On a recent follow-up visit after he had some skin lumps removed, I asked our lovely vet if she could keep him going for many more years. She smiled knowingly and said, "I know, you want him to live forever." That is what it is like for many of us.

Of course, beneath the longing for much more happy and healthy time together is the knowing that there will be a decline and our cherished pet will die—either suddenly, as happened with our previous dog, or by being put to sleep, perhaps after a gradual deterioration in health and mobility. I want to be well prepared in myself so that when it is time to say goodbye I can ensure that the closing moments of his life are as peaceful as possible.

How do we prepare ourselves for such a loss? To start with, by thinking about it, knowing it, admitting it, and ultimately accepting that is what will happen at some point.

My husband and I talk about it openly. We prefix many discussions about points we need to think about with "When Rufus's time comes . . . ". We're preparing our minds, knowing that our hearts will take a lot longer to catch up.

But on the positive side, I make more time for Rufus, I slow down so that I can notice and appreciate his little ways, which I will miss so much when he is no longer here. I let him choose the route on our walks, and if he really doesn't want to go out in the rain, he doesn't have to. It's all part of the process of gratitude for his life—his wonderful character and independent spirit—and preparing for his time of transition. We each need to find our own way through this.

Before going into the many practicalities of preparing for pet loss, here is another person's story illustrating her struggle to accept the inevitable loss of the family pet.

Our little family dog Ares, named after the Greek God of Mars, came to live with us when I was a teenager. I'm now 37 years of age and living in England, but it's difficult to imagine life without Ares as she has been such a constant in our family in Italy where I come from. I see Ares like a sister, always there. We spent most of our time together when I was young, as she came everywhere with me, even riding on my Vespa! She's always been a very affectionate and loving dog. She's like a piece of my soul.

Now the little dog is 19 years old, blind and unsteady following an attack by a Rottweiler earlier in life. Three years ago Ares developed dementia. She continues to live at home with my parents, where she is never left alone; my parents don't see caring for her as a duty, because to us she is family. We think Ares copes with her ailments because she knows the house perfectly and can find her way around. But while in 2016 she recognized and greeted me when I went home to Italy, the dementia has worsened, and last time I visited she didn't recognize me. I think seeing the gradual decline helps me to get used to the fact that she is not immortal.

However, last August she was really ill, and the thought of losing her was just too much. Dealing with death is difficult for me at any time, and I still struggle with the death of my grandmother last year. Although I only see Ares about five times a year, when I visit my family in Italy, I feel desperate about the prospect of losing her.

I can see that Ares was a huge changing factor in our lives; we grew and changed as a family after she joined us. We'd had dogs in the past, but Ares's arrival coincided with me needing to grow up. Through the difficult teenage years I sometimes got annoyed with her, and now this makes me feel guilty. I wish I'd been more tolerant.

My grandfather hadn't wanted a dog to come in the house, but when little Ares turned up she was treated like a grandchild, and he became a different person. I can see how she helped us face our issues as a family, and we all became closer and more tolerant.

I feel more prepared for her dying now than I did a year ago, but it will still be very hard when her time comes, and very hard for my parents and grandfather as they all dote on her. Meanwhile, family life continues around caring for Ares, as we face her impending end. We all hope she will pass away in her sleep, but I want to be there at home should she need to be put to sleep—to say goodbye to Ares but also to support my father who dreads her having to be euthanized.

Now, we'll move on to the practical aspects of preparing for your loss.

2

Talking to Your Vet about Possible End of Life

This is an area that is difficult to consider but immensely important. A good starting place is to talk openly and honestly with the vet staff about end-of-life issues. This will allow you to ask about the things that worry you so that you can be best informed about your pet's condition, what to expect, and what you can do to keep them comfortable during the time they have left.

Remember that the vet team have your pet's best interests at heart and want to do what they can to prevent your animal suffering. They also want to make sure that when the time comes for you to say goodbye, it is an easy and kind death. But they are also there for you, the guardian, to offer guidance as you find your way through this distressing time.

Staff in a well-run veterinary practice will be sensitive and understand that this is a significant and incredibly difficult time for you, so try not to let worry about getting upset in front of them prevent you from talking freely about your pet's condition and their anticipated death. Indeed, the vet team want you to be as settled as possible in your mind about any decisions you make.

Accepting that one's cherished companion animal is nearing the close of their time is a journey in itself, with many twists and turns along the way. Although your mind may begin to see the reality, your heart may be pulling you in the opposite direction. You may feel that surely something can be done to save your pet. And expectations of what the veterinary profession can offer may be raised by the media showing animals undergoing extensive or pioneering surgery.

Part of this journey is being able to face the reality of the situation and accept mentally and emotionally what needs to happen. This first activity is to help you to prepare for the crucial initial discussion with your vet so that you can find out everything you need to know before deciding whether euthanasia is the kindest option for your beloved companion animal. Give yourself some time to think about and jot down what you need to ask your vet.

ACTIVITY: Consulting Your Vet

Here are some possible questions you can use, or you may prefer to write your own. Leave a space next to each question so that you can jot down what the vet says in response.

What I Need to Ask about My Pet's Prognosis

- Can you do anything to help my pet to comfortably live longer, such as surgery or medical treatment?
- What would my pet go through, e.g. how would they feel during the treatment?
- How long do you think the treatment would give them?
- Without any treatment, how long do you think my pet will live before they need to be put to sleep?
- What would you do if this was your pet?

This activity is to help you to gather as much information as possible from the vet team so you can keep your heart and mind focused on what is best for your pet. It will also make it easier to sidestep the pressures sometimes exerted by well-meaning but less informed people telling you what you should and shouldn't do.

When Loss Is Anticipated

Once you know that your pet is nearing the end of their time, free-floating worries and fears can surface because you don't know what to expect as their condition gets worse. This next activity is to help you work out what is on your mind and what you now need to ask the vet team.

ACTIVITY: Finding Out What to Expect as Time Progresses

Make a list of all the things you feel you need to find out. Even though it is painful to articulate your thoughts in this way, write everything down so that it's in black and white and out in the open, ready to discuss with your vet. Don't feel under pressure to list everything at once, as what you need to know may change as time progresses.

A few example questions are given to help get you started, but ignore any that don't apply and add your own. Make sure you leave a space next to each question to jot down what the vet says.

What I Need to Ask

- What should I expect as time progresses?
- What changes may I see in how my pet behaves as they get weaker?
- How will I know if my pet is in pain?
- What can I do about it?
- Are there any side-effects from their medication?
- What will help keep my pet more comfortable?
  (e.g. softer bedding, greater warmth/shelter, special diet, less handling, a quieter environment, and so on)

To recap, this exercise is to work out what you need to ask your vet and to keep a note of what is said so you can refer to it later. Some of it will probably change over time.

3

Resources Needed When Preparing
for the Loss of a Pet

This chapter is for those who anticipate the death of a much-loved pet because of old age, terminal illness, or any other reason. Knowing that a pet will inevitably die can be difficult to face, and these pointers are designed to guide you along the way. Often there is much fear attached to this time, and although there may be many things to "do", it's good to take some time to think about how you, as the guardian, need to "be".

In the circumstances it's easy to be reactive to everything because you don't know what is going to happen next or in the near future. When you feel "on edge" it's difficult to pause and think things through. However, it will really help to consciously try to slow everything down inside, so that your mind can assimilate the necessary facts before you decide how to respond to each situation.

Having a deep inner acceptance that each life has its own time to arrive, grow, live, and finally depart can bring a quiet inner strength and resolve in the face of anticipated loss.

To assist you through the stresses and strains and the many unknown and changing factors, try to keep a focus on the needs of your pet, and what you can do practically to keep them comfortable and relaxed. It's important to remain realistic about what is possible and what you personally can and can't do, so before going any further, let's look at some of the practical aspects, such as what resources may be needed.

Financial Resources

We'll start by looking at the knotty issue of finances. Terminal care requires dedicated time and energy, and costs can soon mount up. However, it can be difficult to consider these issues during such an emotional and potentially distressing time. Funds may be limited, which adds further difficulty when you want to do whatever is possible. So mounting vet bills and possible pet-sitting services (if these becomes necessary) can create additional strain.

Suggestion: ask your vet practice to give you an idea of what it will cost to put your pet through the suggested treatment plan. This may include:

- Consultations (including the cost of out-of-hours emergency call-outs, in case they are needed)
- Investigations (itemized, if possible)
- Any palliative treatment that may be needed
- Medications
- Special dietary foods not covered by insurance plans
- Possible cost of having your pet "put to sleep" at the surgery or at home, if and when this is necessary
- The particular after-death services you would prefer

Then sit down, perhaps with a close friend or family member, to assess exactly what you can afford and the knock-on effect of future debt if you decide to borrow.

If you have insurance carefully check your cover. If this isn't clear, get in touch with the company and ask them to write to you to confirm what is excluded, what will be covered and up to what limit, so that you have the information.

Following this, you may need to speak to your vet practice to discuss what you can and can't afford, which will make them aware that you have limited funds available. Emotionally, this is a challenging area, and can be fraught with contradictions between what your heart feels and what your head says. Your mind needs to be as settled as possible with your plan so that in the times ahead you can look back and see what you decided and why. Without this reasoning, it is all too easy to make snap decisions that you may regret later on.

You may go all out to arrange a loan or decide to stay within a more comfortable financial perimeter because you need to be able to manage in the future. In the end, it always comes down to what feels right for you, but it's worth taking the time to carefully assess the situation so you can make conscious decisions about important matters.

Coping with Lack of Funds to Pay for Vital Vet Care

Life circumstances can change unexpectedly, and people may suddenly find themselves under financial strain. Additional expenses, such as an ever-increasing vet bill, are bound to bring further worry and stress.

On occasion, the suggested treatment is astronomically expensive and way above what could have ever been anticipated. For example, I know of one lady whose young dog required specialist back surgery following an injury; she had been told it would be between £10K and £12K. Thankfully, she did have some insurance and, although it only would cover up to about half of the cost, she had a supportive and loving family who understood what it meant to love a dog, and who could all chip in to help. But if the money hadn't been available this lady would have faced a very difficult situation as the surgery appeared to be the only solution to offer long-term pain relief and normal mobility.

Sadly, there are situations when people simply cannot afford to pay for crucial diagnostic tests and/or treatment for their pets—the money just isn't available, and there is no insurance cover or the policy doesn't cover a particular condition or situation.

If you find yourself struggling with money, have a think about different options that could help without causing you to end up in dire financial difficulties further down the road. For example, friends and family may be able to help with a loan, perhaps with a number of them each contributing a small amount. You may be able to think of simple ways to raise funds, for example, a Facebook appeal, crowdfunding, a small sponsored event, a garage sale, or offering a local service, such as car washing, gardening, sewing, or cleaning.

Whatever your financial situation, it is vital that your pet receives vet care when needed. In an emergency, the first port of call is usually your own vet. Make sure you let the practice know straight away about your financial restrictions so that they are aware you may not be able to pay for expensive tests and long-term treatment. Your vet team should be happy to provide initial, short-term basic care for your pet to ensure relief from pain and suffering in an emergency. If urgent euthanasia from sudden illness or injury is needed, the vet should be able to arrange this without delay.

In less urgent situations, be sure to talk to your vet right from the start if you are struggling financially, so they can discuss options to help you to secure your pet's well-being. If you have been a regular client at the practice and have always been able to pay on time previously, you'll need to let them know about a change in circumstances so that they are aware that funds could be an issue in the future. Your practice may have a policy that allows clients to pay vet bills in instalments. You could ask whether there are any animal charities, such as the PDSA, RSPCA, the Blue Cross, the Dogs Trust, or small, local organizations, that could help. But please be aware that there are usually set criteria as to who can benefit, and most charities require proof of that eligibility.

When there is no financial help available from any avenue, euthanasia to prevent suffering may seem like the only option. Sometimes this can lead to someone considering relinquishing a beloved pet to an animal charity for treatment and subsequent rehoming. Of course, when there is a strong bond between the person and the animal, this is incredibly difficult and heart-breaking. If you find yourself in this distressing situation and are thinking of relinquishment, do contact the charitable organization direct, explain the situation, and see what they can offer. Remember that the people who work in the charities are not there to judge or criticize. Their focus is on animal welfare and doing whatever is best for each individual animal and their guardian.

When you have explored all options, you may come to the conclusion that the kindest thing for your pet is to have them put to sleep, because they are likely to suffer if they don't receive the recommended vet treatment you cannot afford. However, before finally making such a decision, do contact your vet practice to explain your situation clearly. Ask whether there are any cheaper options for tests and treatment that may offer a decent quality of life, one you could perhaps afford with an agreed in-house payment plan. You may also want to consider a second opinion from a different vet.

It is easy to feel like you've "failed" if you face having to put an animal to sleep because you don't have the funds for the recommended treatment; therefore, it is important to know in your mind that you have explored all options so that later on you can look back and realize that you did all you reasonably could in the circumstances to prevent suffering, which is the crucial issue. When people love their animals, they want to do all they can to ensure that they don't suffer, even if that means losing them earlier than anticipated.

Your Time, Energy, and Emotional Resources

People do not always take into account the time and energy that can be involved in caring for a terminally ill pet. If you're retired or have plenty of free time and are in reasonable health yourself, then this is less of an issue. However, if you have a demanding job and various commitments, or if your home circumstances don't allow you the space you need to give your pet the necessary care, this is an area to look at carefully.

I remember supporting someone whose beloved cat was really ill, but whose partner didn't understand and certainly didn't share her deep feelings and concern. It was an extremely difficult situation for the lady. She wanted the best care for the cat but realized that she was limited in what she could guarantee.

She kept her focus fixed on her cat's welfare, and rather than prolonging his life with ad hoc health care and subsequent ineffective pain management, she decided that it was better to ensure that this cherished animal had a kind and gentle death sooner than a more supportive situation would have allowed.

People can, and do, go to great lengths to keep caring for terminally sick or elderly pets. Like people, animals may become physically disabled or mentally affected, both of which can cause suffering. It is generally easier to decide that euthanasia is the kindest option if the animal is obviously suffering from pain or other distressing symptoms which cannot be managed. But more subtle levels can be unknowingly bypassed in the understandable desire to prolong life.

Often a terminally sick animal requires a lot of daily care. Over time, this can become exhausting and stressful—physically, mentally, and emotionally. In such circumstances, because you care, you may simply keep going, and over time, this can affect your own health and emotional and mental well-being. The emotional stress can be immense, especially when you're aware that ultimately you will need to say goodbye to your cherished companion. This, together with the ongoing uncertainty of the situation and seeing your beloved pet go through a stringent medical regime, can take its toll.

The message in this section is that your welfare counts, too. The human–animal relationship is often complex and multifaceted, and both pets and people need to be considered as a whole. There may be an overriding feeling that you cannot let your pet down, so you keep going with an increasingly relentless regime of care, which inevitably can become wearing upon you and your companion animal.

Sometimes you need to pause and reassess the situation, and a chat with your vet can be very useful. Tell them how you are feeling, perhaps explaining your daily caring routine and what you are doing to try and keep your pet comfortable and safe. Don't be embarrassed if you are upset because this is a natural reaction to being under such a strain as well as facing the loss of your much-loved animal.

Your vet team will be mindful of your welfare as well as that of your pet, and will understand that you have to be realistic and practical. They are there to help you review the situation and find the best way forward.

Even when it becomes clear that your beloved pet needs to be gently put to sleep, you may struggle with guilt if you think you're giving up or failing. But, of course, this isn't the reality. What is needed is to recognize when all that could be done has been done, and that it is finally time to say goodbye.

Palliative Care at Home

Some veterinary companies offer palliative medicine and end-of-life care that aim to keep terminally ill, chronically sick, or elderly pets in their home, allowing the guardians to have as much time as possible with their beloved animal until it is time to say goodbye. This involves home visits by a vet to assess the pet's quality of life and levels of pain and suffering so that a care plan can be made, which includes prescribing any medications or intervention needed to keep the pet comfortable. There is usually a 24/7 care line providing online and phone support from the vet team. This service may include making a kit available in case of crisis, such as the pet's condition suddenly deteriorating whilst awaiting an urgent vet visit.

Whether or not to opt for hospice care is a very personal decision, with different weights and balances to consider. There are practical issues, such as if this type of service is available in your area or whether it can be sufficiently carried out under the supervision of your own vet. It will also depend on whether you have the inner resources, money, and capacity to fully commit to whatever might be required over the days, weeks, or perhaps months ahead. Besides the practical aspects, it is about what feels right for your pet, your circumstances, and your own beliefs and values with respect to your pet's transition.

Some guardians embrace the idea of palliative care and take solace in knowing that they are doing everything possible to ensure their pet's comfort while giving him or her as long as possible. Here is an account about caring for a terminally ill cat:

> When my cat Angel was diagnosed with a malignant cancer, a lump growing just below her left ear, the vet told me she would have three to six months to live. I decided I would do everything I possibly could in that time to give her a good quality of life, which included

supplements, immune boosters, and pain medication from the vet. Of course, I was in shock at the news, but what I discovered in the weeks was that the time was a huge gift as I was slowly able to adjust to the fact that my beloved pet would soon no longer be with me. I believe it also gave her time to adjust to the fact that she was going to pass because I honestly believe towards the end she did know.

As it turned out she only lived for another six weeks, but I am so grateful for that time we had together. Being able to hold her and comfort her was such an easement for both of us and continued to build the strong bond we had developed over 14 years. Although very difficult at times, the whole process during those six weeks felt very natural—a time to adjust, a time to continue to love, and a time to say goodbye. I felt very strongly I would know when to call the vet for the end-of-life injection, and I did, taking her lead when no more could be done to ease her pain. Looking back I am content to know that I did everything I could for her and so very pleased I let the process take its natural course.

For others, the main focus will be to ensure that their beloved pet has an easy death, avoiding any further suffering or a potential crisis when urgent euthanasia may be needed, such as in the middle of the night or over a festive holiday, making access to a vet difficult. As someone explained after making the heart-breaking decision to arrange to have her elderly dog put to sleep later that day because his condition was deteriorating, "He has only ever had happy memories, and I want it to stay that way."

If you are thinking of palliative care at home for your pet, discuss this with your regular vet who may be able to support you through the process or may possibly recommend a local veterinary company and arrange for the transfer of your pet's medical records. Unless you have unlimited funds available, you'll need to check the potential costs involved, and it is important to know that any veterinary professionals are accredited by the relevant College of Veterinary Surgeons in your country. They may also be members of the International Association for Animal Hospice and Palliative Care (IAAHPC).

4

Creating an Advance Plan
for Your Pet's End of Life

Although it can be very difficult to think about your pet's end of life, looking at the practical aspects in advance and creating a plan can make the process easier for both you and your companion animal. Over the years of supporting people through loss, I have noticed that when a guardian has things in place and has made decisions ahead of time as far as possible, they are able to work through the inevitable loss with greater ease.

Even if circumstances suddenly change, if you have a plan in place it lessens the risk of needing to make snap decisions about important issues that you might regret further down the road. It also means that you can gather information, look into the different options, and take your time to decide on the best way forward while the situation is relatively calm.

Areas to Consider

What follows are brief points about what to include in your plan; further details can be found in the chapters referenced. These ideas can potentially bring up difficult emotions, so if time allows, you may find it easier to approach things gently and without pressure.

Your Personal Resources

- Having consulted your vet about your pet's prognosis, take some time to review your personal resources: finances, time, energy, and emotions. This will help you to keep plans realistic and grounded.
- Another area to explore is your own values and beliefs about what you feel will be right for your pet in terms of palliative and end-of-life care.

  (See Part One: Preparing for Pet Loss – Resources Needed When Preparing for the Loss of a Pet, page 23)

Booking the Euthanasia Appointment for a Small Animal

- When it is time to say goodbye, would it be better for this to be at home or at the vet practice? Many vet surgeries offer home visits, but it is worth checking this, especially if you live in a fairly remote area or the practice is particularly small.
- Another decision to look at is whether you want to, and feel you can cope with, being with your pet when they are put to sleep.

(See Part Two: The Transition – Euthanasia – Coping with Planned Euthanasia, page 49)

Booking the Euthanasia Appointment for a Large Animal

Your vet can help you think about these important issues:
- Which would be the best method to use to put your animal to sleep?
- Do you wish to witness the procedure, or to say your final goodbye beforehand and leave your animal in the trusted hands of the professionals you have employed?
- Where would be the best place, ideally peaceful and private, with easy access, for the collection service you plan to use after euthanasia?

(See Part Two: The Transition – Euthanasia – Euthanasia of Large Animals Such as Equines, page 53)

Whether to Request Sedation before Euthanasia

- Some vet practices give sedation as a matter of course but not all do so, and the need for sedation can depend on the animal's condition and how they generally cope with medical intervention. Therefore it is worth discussing this with your vet in advance to see what they offer and what they advise about your particular pet.

(See Part Two: The Transition – Euthanasia – Coping with Planned Euthanasia, page 49)

What to Take or Have on Hand for the Appointment

- Think about what would be comforting for your pet as they are put to sleep, for example, their blanket and/or other items with familiar scents.

(See Part Two: The Transition – Euthanasia – Practical Aspects and What to Expect, page 52)

A Chance for the Family to Say Goodbye

It may not be possible for everyone to have the opportunity to say their personal goodbye, but it is important that they each understand what is happening and why it needs to happen. This could be:

- Young people who are away at university
- Children at school
- Family members who are working away from home

(See Part Two: The Transition – Euthanasia – Coping with Planned Euthanasia, page 49)

Preparing Children for Pet Loss

- How to do this depends on the age and the capacity of each child to understand and cope with the concept of dying, and also the depth of the bond they have with the pet.
- If time allows, you can gently introduce them to what is happening in line with your thoughts and beliefs about death and dying.

(See Part Five: Other Aspects of Pet Loss – Children and Pet Bereavement, page 107)

Special Requests

- Do you want to request a snippet of fur or a loose feather as a special keepsake? If so, you'll need to let the vet know before or at the time of their transition.
- It may be possible to have a paw print taken of a cat or dog, either before or after the pet has been put to sleep, either by the vet or as part of the after-death service.

(See Part Three: Coping After the Death of Your Beloved Pet – Ceremonies and Memorials, page 68)

Emotional Support

- If you find yourself struggling and want to talk things through with someone who understands, several organizations offer companion animal bereavement support. Your vet practice should be able to advise you or you can search online.
- These services may offer different options, such as online, face-to-face, or telephone support. Generally they are run on a not-for-profit basis and are manned by volunteers who have been through their own bereavement journey and are trained to support others.

- There is a cost if you select a private counsellor in your area.

  (See Resources, page 154)

Taking Care of Your Pet's Remains

- This is potentially another very difficult area to think about in advance. However, planning ahead will help to ensure your wishes are met about how your pet is laid to rest.

  (See Part Three: Coping after the Death of Your Beloved Pet – Taking Care of Your Pet's Remains, page 63)

I suggest that you make a list of which points apply to your situation and approach this difficult process in small and manageable steps. Even if events overtake your plans, if you have given some thought to these important areas, it will go some way towards preparing for what is to come and allow you to feel more in control of the situation.

5

Considering Euthanasia for
Pet Behaviour Problems

Considering euthanasia for behavioural problems is particularly stressful. You may have tried absolutely everything to help your pet but finally reached the conclusion that it is in the best interests of everyone concerned to have the pet put to sleep.

Other than legally enforced euthanasia of animals, the decision rests totally with those who are responsible for the animal. This chapter does not intend to give advice or influence the reader in any way; what is written must be seen only as aspects you may wish to consider within the weights and balances of your own decision-making process.

Firstly, it is incredibly stressful for guardians to witness aggressive behaviour in their pet. Often the immediate reaction is to get the animal to the vet and request euthanasia for fear of them inflicting further damage. This reaction is totally understandable because everyone has to ensure that no one is injured or seriously threatened by any animal in their care.

It is worth looking at whether we *react* or *respond* during stressful events, because these can have totally different outcomes:

Reactivity is immediate, adrenaline driven, and often triggered by fear, upset, shock, or anger. It's what we do without thinking, and it leads to snap decisions.

Responding is more measured and slower, allowing time to take on board what has happened and to think clearly about the situation. It means we can weigh the situation and reason things through before making an important decision.

We may later regret making a snap decision about euthanizing a pet that has reacted aggressively when it becomes clear that the reasons for the unexpected and out-of-character behaviour were not fully explored. For this reason, in order to get a fuller picture, sometimes animal behaviourists suggest that guardians safely and humanely contain the pet to avoid further incidents and give themselves 48 hours to calm down after the worrying event.

A timeout allows you to think things through, away from the pressure and opinions of other people, and to seek professional advice so that you can understand the cause of the unwanted behaviour before responding. For example, on reflection it may become clear that the animal was put in a situation in which it couldn't cope so it reacted from fear.

The standard advice in animal care is to avoid assumptions and ask a vet to make a thorough examination of a pet when there are any sudden or gradual changes in behaviour, as there may be a physical reason. For example, a horse or dog deemed dangerous or uncontrollable may be suffering pain from an undetected injury or underlying illness.

Your vet may refer you to a suitably qualified and experienced animal behaviourist to further assess the animal so that you can make an informed decision about your pet's future. Alternatively, you can find a suitable behaviourist through accredited UK organizations such as those listed below. Be sure to ask whether the trainer or behaviourist has experience in, and a proven track record of successfully working with, the relevant issue:

- The Animal Behaviour and Training Council (ABTC)
- The Association of Pet Behaviour Counsellors (APBC)
- The International Association of Animal Behaviour Consultants (IAABC)

Pet behaviourists and vets have the unenviable task of recommending euthanasia when no satisfactory solution can be found within the given circumstances. Having the animal rehomed may seem an easier or better idea on the surface, and will distance you from the difficult decision about euthanasia, but ultimately securing the kindest and safest option for the pet is the priority, even if this means having them gently put to sleep.

Sadly, when animals deemed to be dangerously aggressive are passed on to someone else, they usually take their problems with them, and once they are no longer in your care, you have no say in how they will be treated and whether they will be subjected to abuse. Some rescue centres are unable to take dogs with a bite history. Those that are able to accept them with a view to rehabilitation will probably have many dogs awaiting forever homes that do not have a history of having bitten. Consequently, the animals with complex behavioural problems are likely to have to wait longer in what can be an extremely stressful and unfamiliar environment.

If the behavioural problem is non-aggressive, such as severe separation anxiety in dogs, or incessant screeching in a parrot, then rehoming to a family or welfare organization that can offer specialized and sensitive care may be a possibility. This would need a full consultation and assessment by a veterinary professional and/or animal behaviourist, who could consequently offer advice and possibly refer you to a suitable sanctuary or rehoming centre that has the capacity to rehabilitate your pet before finding them a forever home.

If your pet came from an animal rescue organization, check whether they offer support and/or assessment of behavioural issues, as they may be able to help with advice and guidance.

In Conclusion

To reiterate, when considering end-of-life issues for pets, it is important to always keep in mind the question, "What is best for this animal?" This applies whether the pet is terminally ill, severely injured, deteriorating due to old age, or suffering from behavioural problems for which no appropriate solution has been found. Understandably, it is incredibly difficult to lose an otherwise healthy pet due to behavioural problems, but knowing that you explored all options and sought professional advice before agreeing to euthanasia can offer some reassurance during this stressful time. It may help to remember that securing a compassionate death can be a final act of kindness, however difficult it is for those left behind.

6

Finding the Right Time
to Say Goodbye

People often say to those going through this process, "Oh, you'll know when the time is right." Certainly, you may know at the point; however, trying to decide when to have a much-loved companion animal put to sleep can present a myriad of uncertainties. Because of the emotional and mental turmoil, it can be difficult to quieten your mind and listen to your instinct. On the one hand, you want whatever is best for your pet; on the other, this is an irrevocable decision.

You may worry about having your pet put to sleep too soon and, therefore, depriving them of time. Or you may be anxious to ensure that they don't get to a stage when they start to suffer. The thing to remember is that you don't have to work this out totally on your own. While the final decision has to be made by you, the vet professionals are there to offer vital information and guidance.

One way of thinking about when to consider euthanasia is that it is *preventing* suffering rather than *ending* suffering.

I remember a few years ago going through this myself with an elderly guinea pig. Beryl had been a wonderful companion who had played a crucial role in educational sessions for a school programme called "Being Kind to Animals", before retiring at around four or five years of age. When she reached the grand age of eight years, which is good going for a guinea pig, I noticed some changes in her demeanour and body condition that made me think she wasn't feeling as well as normal.

I was determined that this little life wasn't going to suffer unnecessarily, and am firmly of the mind that a little too soon is definitely better than a little too late. So I took her to the vet for a checkup and asked outright whether I needed to consider having her put to sleep in the near future. I explained that I was anxious to ensure that she didn't suffer; she'd had as comfortable a life as I could offer her, and I wanted to ensure that she had a comfortable death. The vet gave her a thorough examination and reassured me that she was in good health and would probably go on for another year! She also told me what to look out for that would indicate that Beryl was losing condition.

I was pleased and relieved and arranged to take her every six months for an assessment, or sooner if I had any concerns. A year later, Beryl's condition suddenly deteriorated, and despite the fact that she kept eating, I knew that it was time for her to be gently put to sleep. The vet agreed, and I said my goodbye to this beloved guinea pig who had reached the grand age of nine.

My point in sharing this story is to show that rather than inwardly fretting and worrying, I discussed my concerns with the vet and got professional guidance and information, then, having been reassured, I was able to enjoy the time we had left together.

Here's another story to help illustrate how a friend worked out the best time to say goodbye to her beloved cat.

> *My friend's cat, Silver, became suddenly ill, and after consulting the vet and exploring all the options, she knew that the kindest thing was to arrange for him to be put to sleep. She was then faced with the difficulty of working out the right time, as although it was clearly imminent it wasn't quite the right time at that point.*
>
> *To reduce stress for her cat, she wanted a home visit for the euthanasia and, ideally, this would be with her usual vet. Originally, she booked the appointment for the Friday, but as the day dawned, she knew that it was a little too soon. It became clear that the time to say goodbye to Silver seemed likely to fall on the weekend. When she cancelled the Friday appointment she was told that her vet could come out on the Saturday, but if it was Sunday, it would mean taking him to an emergency service, which was likely to be really stressful, especially as it would be a vet neither she nor Silver knew.*
>
> *After thinking things through and weighing the pros and cons, my friend made the difficult decision to rebook the euthanasia visit at home on Saturday. Although it might be a day early, she felt it was more important to keep her cherished cat as calm and peaceful as possible, which she could only do at home. She didn't want to risk the potential additional stress of taking him into a vet hospital on the Sunday or keeping him alive until the Monday if he was suffering.*
>
> *Afterwards, she reflected to me that she felt okay about the timing of Silver's euthanasia because the most important thing was to make his passing as calm as possible.*

There is no doubt that it is incredibly difficult to be objective about your pet's quality of life when emotions are running wild; therefore, a methodical system to gather information will help you stay grounded and be realistic. Keeping a diary of your pet's general condition and behaviour will enable you to keep track of any changes that may not be obvious when you see them every day.

This next activity is to help you to work out a system to recognize important changes as they occur and know what to do about them.

ACTIVITY: Recognizing Important Changes in Your Pet's Well-being

Ask your vet for guidance on how to measure changes in your pet's well-being. The list below offers suggestions, but it will depend on the type of animal and what you and your vet decide about your particular pet's needs. Leave space beside each point to write down what to do:

What to Look Out For

- Behaving differently, such as:
  » Having out-of-character reactions, such as aggression
  » Being listless
  » Avoiding people or hiding
  » Being disoriented or confused

- Are they:
  » Losing weight?
  » Off their food?

- Should I take a photo each week to notice gradual changes?
- Does their fur or feathers look any different?
- Have they got any new lumps or bumps?
- Are they struggling to stand up or lie down, or finding it difficult to walk or move about?
- Are they coughing or being sick?
- Are they crying, moaning or breathing heavily and/or quickly?
- When would I need to contact the vet urgently?
- There may be other things which you or your vet could add to this list.

This focused and practical approach should give you some peace of mind, as you are more likely to recognize a gradual or sudden worsening of your pet's condition and will know what to do about it.

In addition, you'll need the following information written down:
- Normal opening times of the surgery
- Out-of-hours contact details for your vet
- Cost of an emergency call-out

Some Pets Hide Their Illness

Some types of pets will naturally try to hide any signs of illness or weakness, making it much more difficult to notice when something isn't right. Whilst my pet dog will look at me with his paw raised because he has hurt his leg and wants some help, it was a different story when I cared for birds. Generally my budgies, cockatiels, and parrot only showed signs of illness when the disease or condition had advanced and they were no longer able to hide it, by which time they were already very sick. Such masking of weakness comes from an ingrained survival instinct in species that could become easy pickings for potential predators in the wild.

People who look after birds are usually aware of this and keep a keen eye on their feathered charges. It's not just birds that do this; many types of animal have a similar survival mechanism. For example, donkeys have an incredibly stoical nature, and early signs of illness are difficult to notice because they don't show it in the same way as other equines.

Despite keeping a close eye on my beloved avian companions, I discovered that they were very good at hiding the fact that they were unwell. When my parrot became ill, the only thing I noticed was that her breathing seemed faster. Within hours, this had advanced to her breathing being slightly laboured. Despite prompt treatment from a visiting vet at home, and then being treated in the vet hospital, sadly she didn't make it.

On reflection, I realized that there was absolutely no point in giving myself a hard time because I and the avian vet had done everything we could to save her within that short time span, and I had to accept that this is what can happen with feathered friends.

7

Coping with Fears and Emotions

S taying busy caring for a sick or elderly animal can at times take your focus away from personal feelings, but fears and strong emotions naturally arise, often in the quieter moments when you reflect on what is happening. Because the grief process starts before the actual loss, there are bound to be times when you feel incredibly upset at the prospect of your pet's death. Although it is understandably painful and difficult, don't try to hide or stifle emotions; instead, allow them to surface and be released as and when you can.

Emotions naturally play a crucial role throughout the grief process: before, during, and after a loss. Anyone who has experienced a significant loss will know how incredibly powerful and destabilizing they can be. I remember feeling like I was drowning in emotional pain after losing a most precious rescue dog. It was as though I was standing in the ocean with my feet just touching the sand below whilst massive waves rose up and crashed down right on top of me.

Being at my wits' end, I recall how I grabbed the phone to contact someone whom I knew was an incredible counsellor and support to people through the whole end-of-life process. I was struggling to stay afloat in the overwhelming waves of my emotions, but her calm voice and compassionate understanding threw me a lifeline.

She reminded me that emotions are finite, and in that instant, I realized that after each overwhelming wave, there was a short period of quiet. These brief moments became my oasis of sanity, and I learnt to use them carefully to lift myself up for a little while and focus on the value and gratitude of having shared ten years of my life with such a marvellous little companion. Gradually, the waves of emotion became smaller and less frequent, and although it remained difficult to cope with the emotional roller-coaster my life had suddenly become, I knew that in time I would work through it and come out the other end.

Try to be aware of your stress levels, and remember that, as the carer, you also need to receive care. If you have friends or family who understand that you're going through a difficult time, allow yourself to accept their love, support, and, where appropriate, practical assistance. If you aren't able to draw upon others in this way, there are some excellent organizations that offer a listening ear, understanding, and support to people before and after pet loss. No one has to go through this totally alone; support can be found by searching on the internet for "pet bereavement support".

Besides worrying over the many practical issues, you may find you have numerous free-floating anxieties about your impending loss, such as:

ACTIVITY: Identifying Free-floating Fears

As difficult as it seems, it's useful to identify and name each worry or fear, so that it is out in the open rather than rattling around inside your head alongside numerous other issues you are trying to cope with. Once it's out in the open you may begin to look at what you can do, if anything, about each one. Remember that you are going through an incredibly difficult process and, as well as caring for your much-loved pet, it is important to look after your own well-being.

Take some private time to think about what you're frightened of, and jot each one down. You may want to create your own speech bubbles, as below.

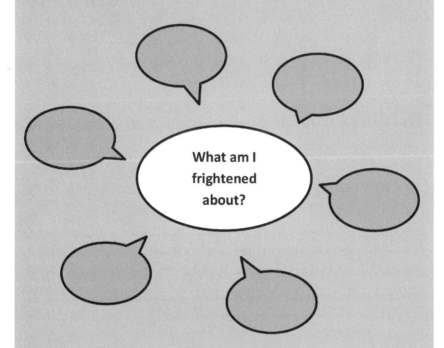

Having identified all these worries or fears, have a think about whether there is something you can actually do to settle your mind on some of these issues, and write them in the spaces you create. If it's easier, just jot them down on bits of card or pieces of a sticky pad or paper.

For example, if you are frightened of being alone with your grief, is there a close friend or relative in whom you can confide? Do you want to get in touch with a pet bereavement support organization through the internet, or perhaps some worries could be allayed by talking to one of your vet team.

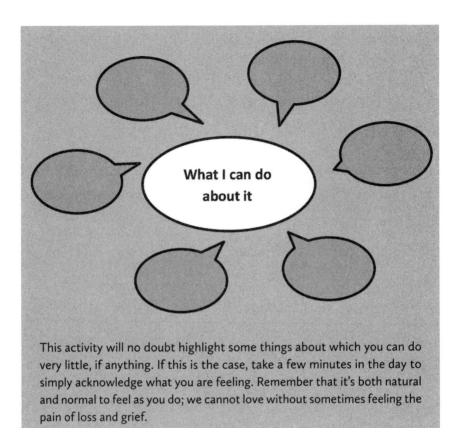

This activity will no doubt highlight some things about which you can do very little, if anything. If this is the case, take a few minutes in the day to simply acknowledge what you are feeling. Remember that it's both natural and normal to feel as you do; we cannot love without sometimes feeling the pain of loss and grief.

Settling your mind on some of these issues will facilitate a calmer atmosphere in the home, which can only benefit you and your pet, enabling you to make the most of the time you have left together. This is important because, if circumstances allow, it helps to slow down and consciously share some special time with your pet whilst you can.

And now, before we continue further, here is a short and simple exercise to help you to pause and breathe.

ACTIVITY: One-Minute Breathing Exercise

You can do this exercise lying down, sitting, or standing, and no one will know you are doing it. It helps to bring a sense of calm, whilst sending signals to your mind and body that it is safe to slow down and relax. The more you practise it, the easier and more familiar it becomes.

- Stand, sit, or lie down.
- Take a slow in-breath through your nose and then release it slowly.
- Breathe in for a count of three, and out for a count of five.
- Allow the air to flow into your chest on the first breath, your stomach on the second breath, and finally your abdomen on your third breath.

Breathe in for the fourth time into your abdomen, hold your breath for a count of two, then exhale slowly.

PART TWO

· · · · · · ·

The Transition

8

Euthanasia

This chapter covers different aspects of euthanasia. Although this can be incredibly difficult to read and think about, it helps to understand what happens during your pet's transition and to consider any options that are available. Having recently been through this process myself I must say that I was glad that I knew what to expect when my own little dog went through his transition. The chapter includes stories from other guardians about their personal experiences of having their beloved pets put to sleep.

Coping with Unexpected Euthanasia (Sudden Injury or Severe Illness)

There isn't always time to prepare and think ahead, such as when a pet has been involved in an accident or has become suddenly severely ill. Of course, this is deeply shocking. In these circumstances, most likely your decision will be based on what the veterinary professionals say is, in their view, best for your pet.

There may be options of major surgery or other life-saving approaches to consider in a last-ditch attempt to prolong life, when you'll need to discuss with your vet what is involved and the possible outcomes. If the animal is in severe pain that can't be controlled, then the decision to end their suffering without delay becomes clear.

During an emergency, there isn't always time to consult the whole family about the need for euthanasia; therefore, not everyone may get a chance to say their goodbyes. In this case, you may want to ask your vet for advice on how to explain the situation to your family, including any children, so that everyone is as clear as possible in their mind. The vet staff may also be willing to explain to the others later what has happened. Understanding why the decision for euthanasia had to be made so quickly will at least help to bring some clarity in a traumatic situation.

Coping with Planned Euthanasia

This chapter will help you be as prepared as possible when euthanasia becomes necessary. Although you realize that your pet's life expectancy is generally much shorter than your own, as your companion animal starts to grow old or struggles through terminal illness, understandably you begin to fear the end.

As the pet's guardian, you naturally feel responsible for their welfare and comfort throughout their life, and increasingly so as they draw towards the close of their time. Everyone hopes for a peaceful and straightforward ending and, fortunately, with veterinary intervention, this is usually possible.

Even though we know that euthanasia is a way of preventing unnecessary suffering (one translation of euthanasia is "easy death"), it is difficult to come to terms with the fact of making such a decision when it comes to your own much-loved pet. Whilst it's challenging enough to get your head around having your pet put to sleep, it is important to consider after-death services. I will expand on this in the following chapter, but mention it here because thinking ahead means that your wishes for laying your pet to rest will be honoured and not be a source of regret later on.

Unless it is an urgent decision, it is important to try to allow all members of the family the opportunity to say goodbye to the pet beforehand. This includes young people who are at university or anyone working away from home. There may be someone who was involved in your pet's care who would want to say their personal goodbye, if possible, or at least know what is happening.

When there are young children in the family, it is best to be honest with them about what is happening so that they are not shocked afterwards to find that their animal friend is no longer there. Phrases such as "being put to sleep" can be disturbing for young children, who may later worry that going to sleep means never waking up again. The chapter Children and Pet Bereavement gives more ideas and information on this.

Things to Consider about Euthanasia of Small Animals

You'll need to think about whether it would be better to take your pet to the surgery or ask the vet to do a home visit, providing your practice does offer the home option. Again, this needs to be discussed in advance, if possible, bearing in mind that it is usually more expensive to have the vet come to your house.

To help you to decide, think about how relaxed your pet is when you visit the vet practice. If they get anxious, you may decide to opt for a home visit. If that is not an option, perhaps you could ask whether it is possible to give your pet sedation at home beforehand.

If you decide on euthanasia at home but your own vet is unavailable to do it, you could ask them if they can recommend another local vet who would be able to do this. If you choose to find a vet through the internet who does house visits, do check everything carefully in advance, including the cost, to ensure that the standard of care and pricing is acceptable to you.

You may want to check with your vet practice about what they offer if you elect to go to the surgery. Some surgeries have a specially designated room for euthanasia, away from the hustle and bustle of the surgery, or they may have a different exit so that you can avoid having to go back through a crowded waiting room afterwards.

The vet will usually ask whether you wish to be present when the final injection is given. There is no hard-and-fast rule; it's entirely up to you. If you know that you will be so distraught it could upset your pet, or that your emotions will totally overwhelm you, you may decide it is better to wait outside and then go in afterwards to say your final goodbye.

Euthanasia at Home

You may want to ask your vet if there is anything you can do at home to prepare your pet. As an example, a close friend of mine carefully shaved areas on her pet's legs where she knew the injection would be given; she did this to more than one site in case there was difficulty inserting the needle at the time of euthanasia. Alternatively, you could take your pet to the surgery a day or two beforehand so that the vet nurse can shave the legs in advance. Sometimes, vets agree to your giving prescribed sedative medication beforehand if the animal is likely to be anxious.

Having arranged a time for the vet to come to your home (bearing in mind that the vet may also bring along a veterinary nurse), try to spend time beforehand with your pet, keeping them comfortable and letting them know how much they are loved. It will help both you and your pet if you can stay as calm as possible, keeping the room quiet and undisturbed, perhaps with peaceful music playing gently in the background. However, do allow yourself to express how you feel, and remember that it's totally natural and normal to cry in response to such a significant loss.

Euthanasia at the Vet's Practice

If possible, take someone with you for support and have them drive you home afterwards. You are likely to feel highly emotional, and having someone who understands what you are going through will help. Vets are very aware of the shock and grief that pet guardians go through and are used to people being upset when their pet dies, so you do not need to feel awkward about showing your feelings. It is understood that this is a very difficult time.

Practical Aspects and What to Expect

This section includes some of the practicalities about euthanasia, in the hope that it will help you to be more prepared.

No matter where the euthanasia takes place—at home, at the surgery, or outside—think about what familiar items may be of comfort to your pet. For a cat or dog, perhaps have a special soft toy or favourite blanket to give them the comfort of something that smells and feels familiar.

You will probably be asked to read and sign a consent form. This can be distressing, but it is a necessary legal formality.

Nowadays, vets will often give sedation before the final injection. This can be particularly useful for small pets, such as cats and dogs, which are likely to need restraining for the final intravenous injection to put them to sleep. An animal might need to be restrained because they are generally anxious, reactive, or highly strung or they get nervous about any veterinary intervention or have recently had a lot of medical treatment.

The sedation injection is given either into a muscle or under the skin using a small needle. This allows the animal to relax prior to shaving a leg for the final injection, which goes into a vein. The idea is that it makes the process as calm as possible, as the animal is less aware of what is happening, and it makes it easier for the guardian to hold and comfort their pet as they gently pass away. Ideally, you would talk to your vet in advance of the euthanasia appointment so that they can accommodate your wishes and ensure enough time is allocated. However, your vet might advise against sedation for medical or other reasons.

If you have decided to stay with your pet during euthanasia, ask the vet to explain what will happen so that you are as prepared as possible. Vets usually give an injection either straight into a vein, or through a carefully placed small tube that is secured into a vein. To do this they will need to shave a little fur. The vet may apply numbing cream to go on the pet's leg beforehand to lessen the sensation of the needle; again this is something you can request if you feel it would help your pet.

The final injection quickly causes unconsciousness and the heart to stop beating. As the pet slips away there may be some muscle twitching, which is a natural reflex action, and a gasp. It is helpful to have a towel or cloth to wrap around your pet, as there is usually soiling after death which happens because muscle tone is lost. Again, because the muscle tone is no longer there, the eyes will remain open once the pet has died.

Euthanasia of Large Animals, Such as Equines

Your vet practice will be able to give you information on options for euthanasia of larger animals, such as equines, so you can decide on which method is best for your beloved animal and your circumstances. As with smaller pets, where possible it is much better to plan ahead to minimize stress and keep things as calm and peaceful as possible. Unless euthanasia has to be done as an emergency to prevent acute suffering, there are practical matters to be considered in advance, such as the method, the place, and taking care of the animal's remains.

There are two different methods of equine euthanasia. The first method involves an overdose of anaesthetic injected into a vein in the neck, which will make the animal quickly go unconscious and cause the heart to stop beating and breathing to cease. This may involve putting a cannula (small tube) into the vein and securing it ready for the final injection, or alternatively the drug may go direct into the vein, depending on what the vet assesses to be best in the circumstances. Some vets will give sedation beforehand to make the animal as relaxed as possible. If this is something you think would help your particular animal, discuss it with the vet, ideally in advance of the appointment.

Alternatively, the vet or an experienced and skilled marksman who has a current firearms licence can use a humane pistol. This will cause immediate unconsciousness and death. Again, sedation can be given beforehand, but as this can only be administered by a vet it would need advance planning if a marksman is being employed.

Whichever method is selected, you will need to know the cost and be fully confident in the proficiency and humane handling and care of your animal during their transition. Personnel administering euthanasia for large animals should guarantee a high standard of animal welfare, whilst demonstrating a sensitive and understanding attitude to the guardians. A personal recommendation from other members of the local equine-loving community can be very useful in this regard.

Practical points to consider include choosing a location out of sight of other animals with a soft surface, such as grass or bedding. The area also needs to be accessible for the vehicle used to collect the body afterwards.

Providing your equine companion is still eating, it might be possible for the vet team to offer them a ginger biscuit or other favoured tasty treat when being put to sleep by injection.

As noted above, staying with your animal during euthanasia is a personal choice, but you need to be aware that it is highly unlikely that you will be able to be close to your companion at the actual point of administration of the drug or humane pistol because of health and safety considerations. The euthanasia of standing equines will involve the animal falling down, which is particularly sudden when a humane pistol is used. You would need to be mentally and emotionally prepared for this, and any associated sounds and sights that you are likely to witness should be explained to you beforehand.

In professional hands, and with kind and knowledgeable handling, euthanasia causes immediate loss of consciousness for the equine, thereby preventing suffering. As with smaller animals being euthanized, there can be a gasp, muscle or leg twitching, and their eyes will stay open. When a humane pistol is used for euthanasia, be prepared for visible blood loss.

Understandably, you may feel that you would rather say a final goodbye to your beloved companion animal before euthanasia and leave the professionals to carry out this final act of kindness. If this is the case, you may have a trusted friend who would agree to be present at the time of transition for you, which can be reassuring.

If you intend to use a slaughterhouse it is advisable to ensure that it is reputable. In recent years, the high levels of concern about how animals are handled and slaughtered in some establishments were such that new legislation making CCTV mandatory in all slaughterhouses in England became necessary to help safeguard the animals' welfare.

Euthanasia of Pet Birds and Very Small Animals

Usually, very small caged pets will be taken to the vet to be put to sleep rather than having a home visit. If possible keep them in their usual cage, but if you need to transport them in a different carry cage, make sure that some of the bedding and perhaps some food items from their normal living environment are included so that they are surrounded by familiar sights and scents.

Euthanasia of pet birds and very small animals such as guinea pigs and hamsters is different because their veins are too small for an intravenous injection. It has to be said that some methods are considered kinder than others, and I would always ask the vet to explain the procedure.

Avian vets are most likely to use anaesthetic inhalation gas, to which birds are particularly sensitive. This will cause them to fall into a deep sleep and pass away peacefully. This is a method I would insist on for any companion birds that were in my care. Injectable methods for birds and very small animals involve a needle that has to be quickly passed into the heart. Some vets will sedate little pets with a dose of inhalation anaesthetic gas first, which again is something you can request or insist on for your pet.

Other euthanasia methods may be used but you need to understand them and be sure these are acceptable to you before giving your consent.

Note about "gassing": If a vet says that they'll give your pet gas to put them to sleep, ask them what sort of gas. Most likely they are referring to anaesthetic gas, which causes unconsciousness, as described above. But please be aware that another gas, carbon dioxide, CO_2, has been used for killing rodents and birds, particularly in research centres. Carbon dioxide causes suffocation, which takes around three minutes of the animal gasping desperately for air, something a guardian would not want for their beloved pet. If carbon dioxide is proposed by a vet, please consider taking your pet elsewhere to ensure a kind and humane death.

Euthanasia of Exotic Pets

If you care for an exotic pet, such as a lizard, snake, or tortoise, you will most likely already use a vet who is experienced in treating your type of pet and knowledgeable and proficient in end-of-life care. However, for your own peace of mind, do not hesitate to ask them how they would euthanize your pet so you can be sure that it is as humane and painless as possible. There are specific methods for fish, which again you would need to discuss with your vet.

When Euthanasia Is Not Straightforward

Although euthanasia is designed to ensure a quick and easy death, it has to be said that occasionally things don't go as planned. This may be due to the animal's physical state having declined to the point when the usual procedure becomes technically more challenging, or the pet is difficult to handle because they are stressed or in pain. Sometimes, the injection itself can sting as it goes into the vein, and an already stressed animal will naturally react by crying.

Any of these scenarios are incredibly upsetting for the guardian and stressful for the vet team. If technical difficulties arise, everyone needs to remain as calm as possible and look at the options to make things easier for the pet. One option may be for the vet to administer a sedative and allow time for this to work before trying again. Don't be afraid to say that you want things to be done slowly and calmly and that you wish to pause and talk through how best to proceed. For example, it may be more comfortable for a small animal to lie on a soft bed or blanket on the floor, rather than be firmly held on the surgery table.

If the vet decides on a different method of euthanasia than originally planned, ask them how it works, what it will cause, and how long it will take, so that you know what to expect. Don't be afraid to voice your concerns, and ask for further clarification if you are unsure about what is being proposed.

The Vet's Perspective

Performing euthanasia can be stressful for everyone concerned, including the vet personnel. They carry a huge responsibility as they try to ensure that the process is as calm and peaceful as possible. When things are not straightforward, the pressure they come under is immense. As well as the technical procedure, they also have to be mindful of the distress that the guardians are going through. Furthermore, the vet team may have bonded with the animal themselves so it can be upsetting for them as well.

Payment for Euthanasia

To avoid any misunderstanding, make sure you have an idea of the cost beforehand. It's difficult to have to consider this at such a time, but payment may be expected straightaway, although some practices send an invoice later to their regular clients.

If you have decided to use one of the mobile vet services available via the internet to have your companion animal put to sleep at home, ask for a quote beforehand so that you won't be faced with an unexpected high bill to pay afterwards. Although cost may be the last thing on your mind at such a distressing time, it is a good idea to check out this practical issue to avoid any further upset, and to print the quote so that you have it in black and white, if it is needed.

How You May Feel Immediately after the Death of Your Pet

Even though death was expected, you may feel shocked and distressed once it has actually happened, so do allow yourself some quiet time afterwards.

The sudden and unexpected death of a pet can be particularly shocking, and it is really important to make sure that there is time to recover from the shock before trying to resume normal activities, such as driving or anything for which you need to be fully alert and aware.

9

Natural Pet Death

It's safe to say that most guardians wish for a peaceful and natural death for their beloved pet, ideally that they quietly "slip away", perhaps having fallen asleep and not woken up again.

As we know, animals can die from a number of diseases and conditions in the same way as humans can, a fatal heart attack being a prime example. I lost a most special canine friend in this way, but following the understandable emotional shock of losing him, I was able to take comfort in the fact that his death was quick and that he had led a full and happy life until the very end. However, in different circumstances, I would have had no hesitation in agreeing to euthanasia to ensure a quick and kind death for this beloved pet.

Unfortunately, animals can die suddenly from trauma, such as a road traffic accident or other injury, which may be accidental or occasionally from a wilful act. Having lost a small rabbit in a dog attack, I can understand the shock and sick feeling that such a traumatic death brings.

Witnessing the traumatic death of a beloved companion animal is particularly shocking for the guardian. The images from the incident can imprint on your mind and cause flashbacks, which is obviously very upsetting. Sometimes, people describe reliving what happened as the images of their pet's final moments flash into their mind. Ideas on how to cope with this are given in Part Three: Coping After the Death of Your Beloved Pet. When pets die suddenly, we often need to understand what happened and why. Naturally, the hope is that the death was instantaneous so that the beloved animal didn't suffer for any length of time. Vets can sometimes tell us more about an animal's death by what injuries they sustained and by any eyewitness reports of the incident.

A friend of mine consulted her vet after she came home to find that her elderly dog, Mia, had died unexpectedly in the garden. She carefully described the position of Mia's body and some nearby disturbance, which enabled the vet to give her a couple of possible causes of death, with strong reassurance that in either case she would have slipped into unconsciousness very quickly.

Natural Death versus Euthanasia

Sometimes people say they don't want their pet to be put to sleep because they prefer to let them die naturally without assistance. Whilst on occasion, unassisted death can be a peaceful process, a natural death does not guarantee an easy death; therefore, it is vital to understand what the animal will go through if euthanasia is not provided.

Even if drugs are given to relieve pain, please bear in mind that just because the pet doesn't seem to be in pain, it doesn't mean that they are not suffering. It is important to understand that lack of pain does not mean lack of suffering. Suffering can be caused by intense nausea or struggling to breathe, or from the effects of internal organs shutting down. There may be mental distress from physical disabilities, such as immobility and incontinence.

If you are considering a natural death for your pet, please ensure that you talk through the whole process with your vet in advance so that you are aware of what will happen and how your companion animal is likely to feel.

PART THREE

. . . .

Coping after the Death
of Your Beloved Pet

10

Taking Care of Your Pet's Remains

You will no doubt feel distressed at losing a pet who was a valued member of the family, so it is important to take a little time now to think about how you wish to offer a final service in terms of burial or cremation.

This section is of necessity practical in nature, and is designed to guide you towards making the best choice for your situation. Time spent considering this beforehand, perhaps in discussion with all members of the family, can help to prevent regrets later on. Thinking ahead also means you can research what services are available and look into the different costs and standards so you can choose what fits with your particular beliefs and budget.

Sorting out how you want things to be done when it is finally time to say goodbye brings peace of mind, as confirmed by this lady who had to decide where her elderly pony would be laid to rest after his transition:

> I was having a bit of an emotional struggle all summer as I thought I was going to be facing putting my pony down in the autumn, but thankfully, he has a reprieve and is going to retire and hopefully have a few more years yet. Amazingly, the place I have found for him to retire has loads of space, and when it is his time to go he can be buried there, so I feel at peace with the thought of his final days now, as the farm is very quiet and peaceful and I know that when the end does come it will be dignified and I can plant a tree there to remember him.

However, planning ahead isn't always possible, in which case you can ask the vet practice to keep the remains of a small animal in their special cool area to give you some time to think through what you want to do.

Some people prefer to leave everything in the hands of the vet, whilst others want to make their own arrangements or employ the services of a private concern. What follows are a few pointers to help you to think about the different options that are available.

Cremation

Communal cremation, where several pets are cremated together, means you cannot have your pet's ashes returned. However, you can ask your vet to arrange an "individual cremation". Although it is more expensive, it does mean that you can have the ashes returned to bury in your garden, scatter in a favourite place you had shared with your pet, or keep in a casket or special container. Alternatively, you can contact a private pet crematorium that offers a similar service and may also have a Garden of Remembrance, a peaceful place for you to visit in quiet contemplation and fond memory of your companion animal.

Some pet crematoriums have the facilities to allow owners to view the cremation; this is called a "witnessed cremation". The process itself can be lengthy, but some people find it reassuring to witness their pet's remains being handled with respect as they are placed into the cremation chamber.

It is worth visiting the Association of Private Pet Cemeteries and Crematoria (APPCC) website, which provides important information and definitions of after-death services in the UK. They advise pet owners to look beyond the glossy marketing presentation of private firms and explain how to check that the standard of care delivered is as advertised. They also suggest that you make sure you know how your pet's remains will be handled before agreeing to a collection. For example, when more than one pet is collected from each vet practice, the handling becomes very basic.

The International Association of Pet Cemeteries and Crematories (IAOPCC) is a worldwide not-for-profit organization dedicated to advancing the standards, ethics, and professionalism of pet cemeteries and crematories outside of the UK. Its website contains information on individual locations that you can check.

Burial

You can ask your vet for some practical advice on pet burial to find out what is possible and what is legal within your country or state. For example, in the UK, the law only allows people to bury their own pet on property they own (unless there are local bylaws against this), which means that home burial is not possible for those who live in rented or council-owned properties.

The UK legislation about burying equines is more complex. The rules for Wales, Scotland, and Northern Ireland differ from those in England, so you will need to contact the local agricultural department for your area. If you want to bury a horse on your own land in England, you need to contact your local council's animal health office. The burial site of a large pet is required to be a minimum distance of 50 metres from any well, borehole, or spring supplying water used for human consumption or used in food production, which includes private water supplies. The council may ask for a map marking the burial place and have additional requirements.

In the US, local and state governments regulate the burial of pet remains on any property you legally own. The laws and regulations can differ by state, county, or municipality; therefore, before attempting a pet burial on land you legally own, you will need to find out what you can and cannot do. For example, the laws governing the disposal of deceased animals in the state of Washington not only specify what constitutes a "dead animal" but also dictate how quickly the owner must "properly dispose" of the corpse (within 72 hours). Other states may require a shorter time period for disposal. The depth of soil required to cover the remains varies as well. It generally seems to be around 3 feet deep, as is the case in the UK, but the distance of the burial site from a water course may need to be greater.

Australia does not appear to have the same legal complexities when it comes to burying small pets, but it is wise to check with your vet to find out if there are any restrictions, particularly regarding large companion animals.

Health and Safety Issues: Be aware that in some circumstances you may not be allowed to bury a pet for health and safety reasons due to certain medical treatment having been given.

Post-mortem: If your vet advises that a post-mortem needs to be carried out, or if this is required by your insurers, you will need to discuss what is involved with your vet, including the cost, and check what options you will have for taking care of your pet's remains as it is generally not possible to bury an animal following a post-mortem. Occasionally, an owner will ask for a post-mortem to be done to find out the cause of their beloved pet's death. Post-mortems can reveal why an animal died or was suffering to the point where euthanasia was needed, which can help bring closure. This does need to be discussed with the vet beforehand, as the procedure is not always conclusive.

Some websites advise against pet burial because the anaesthetic drug given for euthanasia may pose a danger to wild animals or domestic pets that could dig up the remains. Biohazards are also mentioned, such as communicable diseases or recent radiotherapy. Your vet will be able to advise you whether and where you can bury your pet. Once you have the go-ahead, the main issue will be to create a suitable plot that will remain intact for years to come.

It is advisable to prepare a burial site that will allow a metre of soil (3 feet) above your pet's body, and to place some large flat stones, such as paving stones, or a number of rough stones, over the grave to maintain its integrity. Digging a big enough plot is extremely hard work, especially if the ground is made up of heavy clay soil or is stony, so you may need to organize help to do this. If access allows, a digger will make it much easier if you need to create a sizeable grave on your own land.

Consider wrapping your pet's body in a biodegradable blanket or sheet, such as one made from cotton, silk, or wool, or in a special pet coffin or small cardboard box. When I buried my own very small pet in my garden, I found it comforting to use one of my favourite silk scarves as a shroud when he was laid to rest. Plastic will prevent the natural breakdown of the body, which happens over time, so it is best avoided.

The whole family may wish to be involved in preparing the ground and finding a suitable stone or plant to mark your pet's final resting place.

When burying a pet in your garden, one aspect to consider is how you will feel if and when you move house in the future. Some people find it really difficult when they have to leave behind their beloved pet's grave. One owner remembers how distressing she found moving home for this reason.

> We shared our home with a beautiful rescue cat called Jake, a gentle furry soul, but tragically Jake had a tumour, and we lost him much sooner than anticipated. We brought him home and buried him in our garden alongside a beautiful flowering jasmine. Unfortunately, I could not foresee that I would need to sell my cottage, and it still affects me now that Jake remained in the garden I no longer own.
>
> Whilst I have struggled with this immensely, I do feel that his spirit lives on in my memories and he is always close at heart. Our pets provide us with so much unconditional love, and although loss impacts everyone differently, feelings of despair can at times be overwhelming.

Pet cemeteries are scarcer and more costly than pet crematoriums, but this could be an option if you would prefer your pet to be buried but either you do not have your own garden or there is not enough space to accommodate a grave. Your vet's surgery can advise you on the availability and standard of local services.

The cost of using a pet cemetery can be significantly greater than cremation or a home burial, and there may be an additional maintenance charge, but the advantages are that the staff will prepare the ground and perform the burial, so you avoid what can be extremely hard manual work. Generally, pet cemeteries are well maintained and offer a peaceful environment to visit your pet's grave in the future, although the distance of the cemetery from where you live will need to be considered.

Farm Animals and Equines

If preferred, you can contact a fallen stock service for deceased equines, but farm animals must be disposed of using an approved disposal method for fallen stock.

In some countries, such as the UK, you will need to inform your vet practice and the passport-issuing authority of the death of an equine so that records can be amended.

If livestock dies on your land, it must be collected, identified, and transported from your farm as soon as reasonably practical. And in the meantime, the body needs to be kept away from animals and birds to avoid the spread of any potential diseases.

Generally, there are specific government regulations for the disposal of deceased farm animals other than equines, and information can be found on the government website or through your vet practice. For example, in the UK, it is not legal to bury or burn the bodies of deceased farm animals, including stillborn animals, even if they were kept as pets.

Collection of the Remains of Equines and Farm Animals

Please be aware that witnessing the removal of the bodies of larger animals, such as a horse or pet cow, can be distressing because of the practical issues involved, so you may prefer not to be present during this time. Similarly, if visiting an establishment that disposes of farm animal carcasses, there is a possibility that you may come across vehicles holding large numbers of deceased animals, which again can be upsetting.

Concerning All Animals

As said before, it can be incredibly difficult to think about how to take care of the remains of your beloved companion animal. Information is available on the internet about "disposing of dead animals", which is understandably too graphic for many people. A note about leaving it to your vet: this can mean that your pet's remains are included in a mass cremation process or taken to a landfill. If you want to know what will happen to your pet's body, be sure to ask for this information.

Ceremonies and Memorials

Ceremonies and memorials are, of course, a matter of personal choice and belief. Children often want to arrange a pet funeral in their own way and select special stones, flowers, plants, and mementos for a site in the garden. It can be an excellent way for the family to come together as a mark of respect and remembrance to recognize their mutual grief. Even when the body or ashes of your pet cannot be buried for some reason, having a particular place of remembrance in the garden can bring comfort in the days ahead.

Engraved plaques and stones are available from a number of sources, although you may prefer to create something yourself. One thing that I've done over the years is to find a nice largish smooth pebble and get to work with either paint or coloured felt tip pens. The idea is to write or paint the pet's name on the top side, and underneath to put the main quality of their life, for example, "Bobby" on top with "Loyal" on the underside. Of course, the pebble can be creatively embellished, either with simple artwork or by gluing on shiny sequins or such like. This means you'll have a totally personalized memorial stone that can be placed in the garden or kept inside. Please be aware that although the artwork can be preserved by varnishing the pebble, if it is left outside it will likely peel or fade over time.

Some people prefer to do an online memorial with photos, or you could, when you feel ready, create a photo book. Another idea is to have a photo cushion made with your favourite photo of the pet on the front, which makes for a soft and huggable reminder. Please bear in mind, though, that some people find it too distressing to look at photos of a beloved pet that has only just passed away because the grief is so raw at this early stage.

Other Ideas to Consider

You can ask your vet for a snippet of your pet's fur or hair or a feather as a keepsake, or do this yourself beforehand.

It may be possible to have a paw print taken in clay or ink, whilst the pet is still alive or after their transition. Some vets offer this service, or it may be possible through a pet crematorium. The printed paw prints can be framed or made into a piece of jewellery or put on a mug, cushion, or other item to create a lasting and poignant memorial.

With individual cremation, there are options of different caskets, urns, scatter pouches, or tubes. You can also find eco-friendly products containing seeds of flowers, plants, or even a tree that will gradually be released into the soil.

People sometimes find their own unique way of remembering a beloved companion animal, as can be seen in this account:

> *Earlier this year, I took my German shepherd girls to a beautiful Northumberland beach where many people take their dogs for a long run. As we walked through the dunes, we came across a large bucket with a photo of a lovely and obviously young dog taped to it. Beneath it was a touching note saying that the dog had sadly died but the owner invited any visitor with a dog to take a tennis ball from the bucket and play with their dog in memory of their departed friend, who had loved nothing better than to run on this beach and fetch his favourite toy. The bucket was empty, so obviously many people had taken up the offer, but I played with my girls anyway with their balls and appreciated even more the joy of being with them and having them with me alive, healthy, and full of joie de vivre. I also thought about the young dog that had loved doing this with his remarkable owners and sent warmth and support to them.*

And another guardian found her own unique way of remembering her beloved dog:

I used to take my dear greyhound, Nelson, to visit an elderly man who had become a good friend, and sometimes a much-appreciated adviser on life matters, over the years. Nelson had a particularly endearing nature, especially for a dog who had been treated so badly before he came to live me; he was often referred to as "a real gentleman", as he was quiet, calm, and kind.

When my dog died from medical problems associated with old age, I was devastated. I missed his gentle presence in the home and missed him walking alongside me and being there when I got home from work. But my elderly friend also sorely missed Nelson, because I'd always take him when I visited and the two of them had developed their own bond between them.

Sometime after Nelson's death, I felt I was in the right place in myself to do something special as a memorial to my lovely boy. I had the idea to knit a greyhound and found a pattern for a life-size one! I couldn't wait to buy the wool and get knitting, and I wanted to make it as a gift to present to my elderly friend. It took a long time, but it was ready just in time for Christmas.

As I knitted, I tried to imbue some of Nelson's soul into it—I wanted it to be really special and to look and to feel like him. I tried to capture his natural expression in the eyes— shy and reserved but calmly watching the world go by. I was very excited and also a bit nervous about the finished result. I put my knitted dog on the settee with his head on a cushion—just how Nelson used to relax.

The day he was complete and lying on my sofa, I had to go out and the thought came to mind, Oh, I'll leave the radio on for Nelson while I'm out. Then I remembered that it wasn't the real dog! But strangely this knitted version of my beloved dog somehow held his presence and it felt like he was there.

Some of my friends found it a bit odd, but to me it was a really special way to connect to the dear soul who I missed so much.

11

Coping with Loss from Other Types of Separation

Losing a beloved animal through death is difficult enough, but there is no doubt that being separated from a pet through other reasons is extremely traumatic. This may be because a pet has gone missing, has been stolen, has had to be rehomed for some reason, or as a result of a relationship breaking down. Some examples are given below.

A dear friend recalled how much she missed a companion dog when she went off to college, which was compounded by the fact that she knew the dog pined for her as well. This lady recalls when her childhood cat went missing and never returned:

> Losing a pet is an awful experience, whether it is unexpected or you have had time to acknowledge the inevitable. But not knowing what has happened to them makes the experience much worse. Our older tabby cat disappeared one day and never came home. This was a real shock and a difficult thing to process for the whole family. I had grown up with him (he used to sleep under my cot), and he was a real character. Obviously, we tried all the usual things: going round to the neighbouring streets to check houses, garages, and any other outbuilding we could find, checking in with the local vets (as he was microchipped), and scouring the local area in case he had been hit by traffic. Based on experience, he rarely stayed out and always came home. Years before, even after being hit by a car and being injured, he had still made it back. But this time, there was nothing.
>
> As time went on we gradually adapted to the fact that he was gone, but the way in which we had lost him from our lives never really settled. Although it was always very easy and very painful to imagine the worst that could have happened, years later those thoughts are quickly replaced with the good memories of his independent character, the silly games he broke into without warning, and the love and affection we enjoyed while he was in our lives.

An elderly gentleman told me about his fleeting relationship with a pet dog when he was a boy:

My parents were not particularly fond of animals, and the only previous pet I'd been allowed to have was a white mouse, although that escaped and mated with a wild mouse—being near an old brewery there were plenty of rodents, which did nothing to endear my mother to pets.

When I was about ten years old, which would have been around 1950, my father came home with a small terrier dog, which apparently he bought in a pub. Of course, I was delighted—a pet to love at last! But this didn't go well, either. About two weeks after the little dog joined the family he ran out the front door and went into a neighbour's house, where he promptly peed on their new carpet. My parents were so embarrassed that when I came home from school I was told the dog had gone. I was devastated and still remember it 70 years on. It was only much later in life when I married my second wife who loves all animals that once again I had the pleasure of canine company.

This poem describes the loss of a pet guinea pig stolen from a front garden, where he had been grazing on the lawn under a protective frame.

Bramble

Little guinea pig, I wonder what happened to you,
It really worries me – if only I knew.
Taken from the garden in which you dwelt,
Whoever took you should now have felt,
The fierce protection for you and your kind,
Which I pray reaches the consciousness of their mind.

If you're still alive, I wish you safe and sound,
And if you've moved on, I hope it is peace you have found.

Another incredibly difficult situation is when animals are taken by force by authorities because they are considered dangerous or reclaimed by the charitable organization from which the pet was rehomed originally. I have come across two of the latter situations. In one, the guardians of a newly rehomed dog, with whom they had already strongly bonded, sought advice from the organization he'd come from. His behaviour was reassessed by a member of staff, and as the dog was perceived to be aggressive he was consequently euthanized without the guardians' consent. Understandably, this initiated a legal investigation. The other involved an animal being taken back by a charity that, for some reason, had deemed the current guardian unfit to care for the pet. Both of these unusual situations caused immense distress for the loving guardians.

Any loss or separation from a pet can cause grief, which can be complicated by a number of unsettling factors:

- The constant worry of not knowing what has happened to a pet that has gone missing

- If rehomed, the concern about how the animal is coping and whether all their needs are being met

- If taken by force by the authorities, the worry of how the animal is being treated and whether they will be euthanized.

This book does not cover these situations in detail, because they are complex and generally call for individual professional input and support according to each unique case.

When an Animal Goes Missing

Generally the first 24 hours are crucial, as you are more likely to find a pet within this time. An internet search on "what to do if your (species) goes missing" usually gives some simple and quick pointers, and there are websites dedicated to helping guardians through this incredibly stressful and upsetting time. Sadly, if the pet is never found, there may come a point when the guardians need to decide that they must allow themselves to grieve, and grieve fully, which could include creating a memorial and working through the different aspects of grief that arise.

Having to Rehome a Pet

If a pet has to be rehomed for any reason, it's important to accept that this will cause a grief process and it will be necessary to work through the many emotions the separation causes. Having ensured the best option for rehoming, it is generally considered that a clean break is best, but this will depend on the individual circumstances.

Pet Taken by the Authorities

The distressing situation of a beloved pet being taken by force by the authorities is a legal issue, which will need legal representation. It's worth knowing that in the UK, all animals fall within the 2016 Animal Welfare Act, which requires:

- A suitable environment
- A suitable diet
- Able to exhibit normal behaviour patterns
- Housed with, or apart from, other animals
- Protected from pain, suffering, injury, and disease

Therefore, although guardians won't be permitted to see animals during their confinement, there should be a means to pass on any vital health care information, such as veterinary treatments the animal has been receiving.

In conclusion, if you have experienced any of the distressing situations mentioned in this section of the book, I hope that the chapters on coping with different aspects of grief offer support as you work towards piecing your life back together.

12

A Bridging Story

To take us from the first half of this book into the second half, which will focus on coping with grief, I am honoured to share this special story. This was written and kindly shared by Hildreth Grace Rinehart, who lives and works with her equine and other animal friends in the state of Vermont in the United States:

Each story is unique and special, but Raja the cat is the first to teach me communication from beyond physical form.

Raja was one of a litter of six deposited in an outbuilding on the property we shared with friends—an old Amish village of about 130 acres.

He was the loud one—black, long-haired with clear green eyes. He came to join our family, sort of by default. When we moved back up north, I tried to leave him with friends since we were up to seven cats then! However, he joined us for the move and grew to the age of 15 before he was to become the only animal in our family to be so sick that he needed to be put to sleep. So, here we are, over 15 years of caring for as many of these beloved creatures as we could, and now—for the first time—we must help one of them to die.

It was an aggressive lymphatic cancer, and medicines were not reversing it nor providing enough comfort. It was a clear choice, and we had the assistance of a professional animal communicator, Irene Lane, to find the timing, and a lovely sensitive veterinarian to come to the house when the time was right.

It was a full turnaround for me—from helping him to live and thrive all those years to telling him it was time to go.

In his last week, Raja made his rounds of each dog and cat in the family, having a bedtime snuggle with each in turn.

He stopped eating and could not walk well. He then gave me the message, as Irene said he would, "I'm ready". It was unmistakeable.

His passing was beautiful and brimming with love and support from his humans. It was like dropping off to sleep and then his body gradually shut down over about ten minutes. I held him and felt his essence swirl around his body as he worked out that things were winding down. I then got a gentle message to break physical contact.

I let him go and immediately felt what I can only describe as his essence jumping from his body and then saw a brief glimpse into this beautiful pattern of pulsing, thriving energy, just like a portal opened up and he flew in.

He was gone, and I felt the thread that connects our hearts stretch out with him into this life force, and with it came the knowing that one gift of death is that it joins these heart threads across time and space, connecting us all unconsciously to the very stuff that life is made of, creating a web that is part of the life force itself.

It was stunning to discover how much presence Raja had been to our family until then—a quietly noble heart of the family.

The next part of this beautiful story continues later, when we discuss the phenomena of pet bereavement (see page 128). In the chapters that follow meanwhile, together, we'll look at coping with grief and how to gently but surely find a way through the many twists and turns that this journey can present.

13

Coping with Grief after Pet Loss

When we truly care for a pet, they become an integral part of the family and a deeply loved companion in everyday life. This applies to any pet—be it a cat, dog, bird, guinea pig, equine companion, or any life we care about. Pets return our love in immeasurable ways, offering warmth and companionship, sometimes preventing loneliness and isolation, with each unique individual enhancing the richness of our life.

There is so much we have yet to discover about the depth of the human–animal relationship, but those of us who have lived with and cared for a pet already know and understand how incredibly special this relationship can be.

Let's make it clear right from the start that grief is grief, whether it is from the loss of a human or pet. Remember, we feel the pain because we care. The sudden sense of loss can be overwhelming, bringing a whole roller-coaster of emotions, such as:

* Shock and numbness
* Confusion and disbelief
* Anger
* Deep sadness
* Longing
* Anguish
* Anxiety
* Guilt

And sometimes we fear that we will never recover or feel normal again.

The severity of these emotions can take us aback, even to the point of thinking, "I'm going out of my mind." These feelings and thoughts reflect the depth of pain of separation and, although this is a normal response it can be hard to bear, particularly in the early days of bereavement when everything feels so raw.

It's not uncommon for someone to cry more over the loss of their beloved pet than the death of a person. Perhaps this is because of the purity and simplicity of the human–animal relationship, or because the pet has been the main focus of their life and the recipient of all their love and care over the years.

Grief of any kind is a natural and necessary process. It's a journey we each face at different times during life, and it is certainly not something to simply "get over". Therefore, grief needs to be recognized for what it is: a normal reaction to the loss of a loved one, be that a person or pet.

We need to allow ourselves the time and space to grieve fully, to release the many emotions that arise and talk through the troubling thoughts and anxieties. No matter who we are, it's natural to cry during grief, as tears offer necessary release during this emotionally turbulent time.

Understanding Grief

Grief is a difficult subject but an important one, and understanding the process may help bring some peace of mind during this turbulent time. Because any significant shock, such as news of impending loss or grief, is likely to cause major disruption to the ongoing everyday normality of your life, you may find that your overall sense of stability is temporarily "out of order" and you're left desperately trying to piece your life back together.

Think of your daily routine as being made up of the many facets fitting neatly together like a jigsaw puzzle, forming the overall picture that describes your life.

Each piece is an integral part of the whole, including your relationships and everything you value and care about. Using this analogy, while life carries on normally the puzzle stays intact, and even if one or two of the pieces become a bit loose or worn around the edges, you can still see the picture.

A significant shock, such as the death or the devastating news of terminal illness of a much-loved pet, causes the many pieces of your life to come apart; it's as though the jigsaw puzzle, previously intact, has now been picked up and thrown onto the ground, scattering into separate components. The overall picture, which until now has been familiar, suddenly disappears, along with the security of the normal interconnectedness of your everyday goings-on.

The jigsaw puzzle analogy may help you to understand why you feel distraught and that your life is suddenly "in pieces", and you'll want to know what you can do to get through this very strange and painful process.

We've all heard that grief is a journey and people may go through different stages. What may not be so clear, though, is that it is possible to actively work through the process, gently but surely face the different emotions and fears, and find a way through to a place of settlement in your mind and quiet acceptance.

A Sense of Relief in Bereavement

Sometimes the death of a pet can bring relief. For example, you may have constantly worried whether your companion animal was suffering, or have struggled to care for an elderly or sick pet for some time, which was stressful and difficult, perhaps even expensive and therefore draining upon your resources. After the animal has died that pressure is no longer there, and it can feel like a relief in some ways. Grief is difficult enough to cope with, so if your personal grief journey is tinged with a certain amount of relief, try to accept it gracefully.

Someone described to me the relief she felt after her dog, a large and unusual breed, died. Although she had really loved her dog and had truly cared for her in the best possible way for 12 years, the behavioural and health issues inherent in that particular breed had caused a lot of stress. Certainly, she felt grief at the loss of her beloved canine and missed her a lot, but she also felt relief.

You may feel relief because the animal is no longer suffering, or from knowing that a beloved pet had a kind and humane death. Sometimes relief surfaces later on, after the initial rawness of shock and grief has settled down. Either way, please be reassured that it's perfectly natural to experience some sort of relief during bereavement.

The Seasons of Grief

Another way of approaching grief involves the analogy of the four seasons, beginning with the sense of being plunged into deep winter by feelings of shock.

At first, you'll need time to take on board what has happened. Even when distressing news was expected, the actuality causes shock, bringing with it a sense of disbelief and that "this can't be happening". It is like finding yourself suddenly thrust into the middle of a cold, hard winter, when everything has frozen over and life comes to a standstill. It may feel a bit surreal, especially when the rest of the world around you carries on as though nothing has happened, whilst you feel that your life as you knew it has changed forever.

The shock you experience can make you feel out of sorts and "all over the place". It is a confusing and exhausting time with everything out of sync, and although you may desperately want to find some peace and rest, sleep can become elusive, causing you to generally feel under par.

As you begin to take on board the reality of what has happened you may find yourself overwhelmed by the depth of emotions you experience – rather like torrents of rain filling fast-flowing rivers as the winter snow and ice finally begin to melt with the onset of early spring. These emotions can be overwhelming, and you need to give yourself the time and space to work through them. It is vitally important to allow yourself to feel what you feel, which can be more difficult than it sounds. You may be afraid of the depth of pain you'll experience, or fear that you'll never be able to stop crying.

Try not to censor your emotions, but release them as they arise, which you may prefer to do in the privacy of your own home or in another quiet place. The anguish during grief can cause a lot of tears, deep sadness, anxiety, and maybe feelings of anger, all of which are natural and normal responses. Rather than bottling things up for fear of appearing weak or unable to cope, do recognize that you are going through a significant process, which takes time and effort to work through.

If you find yourself worrying about some aspect of a pet's death, rather than suffer such anxiety alone, it can help to share your feelings and talk things through with someone who you know will understand. If there are recurring concerns you cannot resolve, try writing them down and then think about who you can discuss them with to try to settle your mind.

For example, you may need to arrange to talk to the vet for a few minutes to seek reassurance about some aspect of your pet's end of life, as can be seen in this short account:

> I couldn't get out of my mind that I'd had my wonderful Sonny put to sleep too early because he perked up a bit just as I took him to the vet. My heart was heavy as I phoned the surgery to make the appointment the day before. But as the next day dawned, he suddenly seemed a bit brighter and I caught a glimpse of my beautiful Sonny as he'd been before he got ill. I think the vet saw my hesitation as me not wanting to let Sonny go, but I was desperate to keep him alive longer if he wasn't ready to go. The vet and her nurse got on with it, and before I knew it he was lying there, no longer breathing. I was too upset to ask or say anything at the time.
>
> My friend, who'd been through a few pet losses herself, was great and took care of me for the rest of that day. We talked a lot over the next few days, and she noticed that I kept on about how I'd had Sonny put to sleep too soon. Eventually, she suggested that I contact the vet to ask if I could have a quick word about my cat's euthanasia. I did this, and thankfully, she agreed to see me. It was hard going back to the surgery, so my friend came with me, but it was worth it to hear from the vet how she'd seen without doubt that Sonny had come

to the end of his life and that to prolong it would have caused him unnecessary pain and distress. In fact, the vet said that in her opinion it was absolutely the right time, and if it had been her cat she would have done the same.

I was greatly reassured by this and grateful to both my dear friend and the lovely vet who took a few moments out of her busy day to settle my mind once and for all. Of course, Sonny's death was still really painful to me, but at least I didn't have the awful added guilt and doubt.

It is easy to feel as though you're losing control during this early stage of the grief process. If you find yourself desperately wondering how much more you can take, think of the emotions like waves in a stormy ocean rising up and crashing around you. Know that eventually each high wave has to come back down, giving you a chance to take a breath and regather yourself. Remember that every storm eventually settles, bringing calm in its wake, as indeed will the pain and distress you may be experiencing.

As you begin to gently adjust to your loss, you will find you are able to take tentative steps to re-engage in some of your usual activities. By analogy, this is like the relief of the warmer, drier summer weather after a very wet and windy spring.

However, even in the summer there will still be some rainy days, when you suddenly feel low again and some of the emotions and feelings you thought you'd already dealt with resurface. This can be disconcerting when you were finally starting to make some progress, and then, *wham*, it's like you're back at square one. Be aware that certain things—and often it's the small things, such as a sound, sight, or scent—can trigger a sudden setback. It's okay; this is normal. Often it can be a case of three steps forward and two back for a while, and then three steps forward and one back, but do remember that you are still progressing, slowly but surely. Try to recognize setbacks as they occur, and know that these too will pass and you will be able to once again move forward.

The autumn of grief is about the process of gradually and gently letting go of the pain and distress, a little at a time. This is analogous to autumn leaves that over time slowly change their colours and state before being released back to the earth. As with the trees, this doesn't happen all at once, and it's certainly not a process to be rushed.

That said, one of the hardest things can be "to let go", yet we each need to find our unique way of doing so.

Remember that grief is the other side of caring, and you feel pain because you cared. However difficult it seems at times, know that as you progress gently through the different seasons of grief, there comes a quiet healing and, eventually, reconciliation with the fact that life does indeed move on.

As I said earlier, it's never a case of "getting over it"; grief simply isn't like that, so never feel under pressure, either from yourself or anyone else, to do so. Take your time, and do what feels right for *you*.

It is normal to feel low at times during bereavement because you're trying to cope with having lost such a precious part of your life. However, there may be times when you need to gently but surely lift yourself up from the anguish and sadness—to allow yourself to feel a little lighter and happier, as and when you can. As one lady reflected after the loss of her beloved dog, Max:

> *I was totally distraught for days when Max died, and I cried and cried— on my own, with my husband, on the phone to my friends, and with my sister. But after a while, I remembered how Max used to look at me when I'd been upset. He would look very anxious; he didn't like to see me upset. So I tried each day to not stay down for too long, because I knew Max would want me to start to be happy again. It was difficult to do this, especially at first, as I had started to feel very low, but I wanted to get through this in memory of Max as much as for my own sake.*
>
> *Of course, I still miss him terribly, but now when the sadness threatens to descend on me, I try to focus on the good times we shared, and there were many of these, and then I begin to feel a bit stronger. I think of him running across the field, full of joy, and how he'd love to share adventures with me, and this lightens my heart, making me thankful for the wonderful time we had together.*

Please remember that it is totally normal to grieve the loss of a beloved pet, and through the care you offered to your companion animal over the time you shared together, you helped to make the world a better place for animals.

14

Guilt in Pet Bereavement

Guilt often arrives on its own account to burden us when we are trying to cope with a recent loss. Guilt brings the uncomfortable sense that things aren't quite right and makes us question everything, sometimes over and over in our minds, bringing up "what if", "should have" or "shouldn't have", and such like.

Bereavement—indeed, loss of any sort—causes many feelings, such as shock, distress, anguish, disbelief, and anger, a whole emotional roller-coaster. Our normal every-day routine is shattered, and we face the difficult task of having to rebuild life in a new way, adapting to the changed circumstances, which of course is very challenging. It feels like the rug has been pulled from under our feet, making us doubt and question everything to do with the circumstances leading up to the loss.

It's as though this uncertainty leaves the door open to the unwelcome visitor called "guilt", which arrives with a ton of unwanted baggage that weighs us down with all sorts of negative thought processes, such as:

* Feeling guilty if we stop thinking about the pet we have loved and lost or if we find ourselves smiling or laughing
* Recurring worries about having fallen short in some respect
* Not being able to reconcile the loss
* Feeling a weight or cloud that never seems to lift
* Not being able to move on, or, indeed, that we should move on
* Feeling that we don't deserve to be happy ever again.

What can be done about it? Like all unpleasant things, sometimes you need to bring what you're thinking and feeling right out into the open so that you can see what is really going on. Once you see guilt for what it is you can begin to deal with it.

There may be something specific you can't quite reconcile in yourself. If so, take some time to try and identify what exactly it is; perhaps you can talk it through with a friend, family member, or pet bereavement counsellor/befriender.

Once you understand what is worrying you, think about whether you can do anything about it. For example, sometimes bereaved people find that a short conversation with their vet helps clarify an issue.

When I was supporting a man through the devastating loss of his German shepherd dog, it came up in conversation that he felt guilt-ridden because he hadn't taken his elderly and sick dog to see the "Super Vet" from the TV series, to check out if there was any surgery that would have helped the dog's diminishing immobility and, therefore, given her a few more months, or maybe longer. He felt that he'd let her down and hadn't done absolutely everything possible.

This dog had, in fact, been cherished throughout her life and looked after wonderfully, from puppyhood right through to the age of 12 years. Because he couldn't get past this issue, I encouraged him to contact his own vet to have a conversation about it. Thankfully, he eventually did this, and his vet was able to reassure him that he had done the kindest thing for his beloved dog by allowing her to be gently put to sleep when he did. She explained that any further intervention would only have stressed the dog and, if it had been her own dog, she certainly would not have considered major surgery to prolong life.

Unfortunately, sometimes there can be pressure from people who pass unhelpful comments, such as the person who said to a lady who had her golden retriever put to sleep at nearly 16 years of age, "Oh, I think he had a bit more time left in him." Thankfully, the dog's guardian could see the futility and insensitivity of this comment and therefore was able to dismiss it, knowing that she'd done what was best for her dog.

However, sometimes there isn't a specific issue that causes guilt, but a feeling that somehow one's best never seems enough for such a beloved pet. An important aspect of coping with guilt is to reason through what actually went on and establish a balanced view of the circumstances. It is so easy to fall prey to negativity, when in fact there may be a large number of positive things which aren't being taken into account. This next activity is offered as a way to step back from the emotional turmoil surrounding guilt to get a more objective view.

ACTIVITY: Coping with Guilt Issues

Look back over the time you shared with your pet, and think about the many things you did to make their life as happy as possible.

Take a piece of paper, and draw a circle in the middle. Write your pet's name in this. You can use coloured pens if you have any. Now draw lines out from that circle and draw smaller circles at the top of each line, making some big and some small. In each of these surrounding circles, write a few words about what you did for your pet to make their life as comfortable and happy as possible. For example, you may write "always got them checked at the vets when needed", or "made sure they had the type of food they enjoyed", "bought them a comfy bed or large cage", or "played with or walked them regularly". You may find there is a lot!

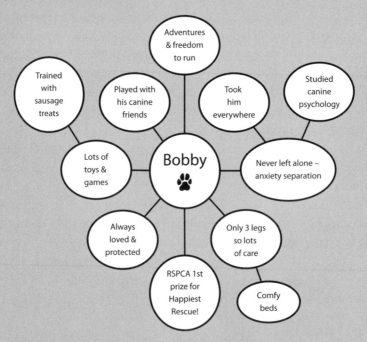

You could include how you helped to settle them in when they were new to your family or how you tried to work through any challenging times.

There may be lots of small, everyday things you did that you never really thought about before, all of which helped create a safe and happy environment for your pet. Write them all down in the separate circles, because they all count. If you're artistically inclined, you could draw little pictures to depict each item, or you could find pictures in magazines or online to cut out and use that depict what you're thinking.

Once you've covered most things, step back from it for a while. Then, later on, take a fresh look at what you've created. Is there anything to add?

Now take some quiet time to gaze at what you have created and absorb the overall impression of how you surrounded your pet with as much care and love as you could. Each time you start to feel yourself being pulled back into the guilt trip, try to pause and think about what you created, which you can see in front of you.

As one lady reflected after working through this activity after the loss of her much-loved cat, Pascal:

> I had a go at the exercise that you suggested on Coping with Guilt. I was indeed surprised at all of the things that my husband and I did in order to give Pascal a comfortable and happy life. It was a refreshing change to brainstorm positive thoughts instead of negative ones. I will keep hold of it to remind myself that in just short of 13 years, Pascal lived like a king!

Understand that guilt serves no useful purpose whatsoever, and ask yourself, "Do I want to spend the rest of my life carrying around this unhelpful feeling?"

15

Anger in Pet Bereavement

Anger is known to be a natural reaction within the grief process. Not everyone feels anger during grief, but if you do, it can be very difficult to cope with.

You may feel angry at yourself, your partner, the vet staff, anyone involved in the death of your beloved pet, or even a higher source, such as God. You may blame someone for what happened or how it happened. You may feel angry and not know why. Or you may simply feel angry at the world at large—perhaps because the world carries on around you as though nothing has happened, when in fact your own world has just fallen apart.

It's important to understand that feeling this way is a normal part of the grieving process, and rather than load guilt onto yourself about it, it's better to look at what you can do about it.

Firstly, recognize anger for what it is: a necessary and sudden release from the increasing pressure of emotions. Anger could be described as strong and overwhelming negative emotions that cause you to feel intolerant, annoyed, and generally "on a short fuse".

Where does it come from? Anger is a readily available emotion, especially when you've lost something precious, or you can't understand what on earth is happening, or you can't do what you want, or you are denied what you most need.

What to do about it? Anger needs to be released *but in a safe way*. So give yourself the necessary time and private space to do so.

Cautionary Note about Releasing Anger

- It is dangerous to take out your anger when driving or doing anything that is potentially hazardous.
- Anger can be destructive and, therefore, needs to be focused away from others, whether that is other people or animals.

Possible Ways to Release Anger

- Punching a pillow
- Going for a run or fast walk

- Taking some deep breaths in and out, exhaling the anger consciously
- Shouting or screaming outside in the open maybe at a tree, the ocean, from a hilltop
- Crying or sobbing without inhibition
- Scribbling down on paper how you feel, and then tearing it up
- Drawing or painting what you're feeling
- Stamping your feet, waving your arms
- Dancing to rock music
- Any other safe activity that releases the adrenalin surges that come with anger.

Unresolved anger can quickly become heated and destructive. If you feel your anger is out of control, or you feel you cannot cope with it, consider seeking the help of an experienced and qualified counsellor.

16

Shocking Mental Images

Witnessing the death of a pet can be incredibly difficult, especially when it was traumatic or shocking. You may find that you keep reliving your pet's final moments, seeing the distressing event in your mind, as described by this guardian whose beloved dog had to be put to sleep because she did not respond to treatment for repeated seizures:

> The downside for me is that I seem to be the one that's still suffering from the loss of Tess; I still struggle massively at times. I have flashbacks of taking her for the last time into the surgery. It all seemed surreal; there I was, holding what appeared on the surface to be a perfectly healthy dog at the time and basically watching her die.
>
> I still wake up in cold sweats haunted by "what if", "why", and "if only".
>
> I was starting to feel quite a bit better about losing my Tess but struggled again recently as I know a guy who had just lost his daughter, aged only 25, through epilepsy; it was like a nightmare returning.
>
> Sometimes I feel I'm getting over it but then bang, something clicks and I'm back into depressive mode.
>
> The best way to describe my world is like I'm on a roller-coaster ride. One moment I'm on a nice easy part of the ride and then, in the blink of an eye, I'm hurtling down this stomach-churning dive.
>
> There's always something that appears, bringing back memories of Tess—some good and some bad. I'll get there eventually, I'm sure. They say time is a healer, but to be honest, I cannot and will not put my Tess out of my memory.

Disturbing thoughts and memories can make sleeping even more difficult, if each time you close your eyes the image replays. The following activity is offered as a way to overwrite the shocking image with one that is positive.

ACTIVITY: Coping with Shocking Images

Consciously think back to a time in your pet's life when they were happy and healthy, perhaps playing or snuggling up with you. You may find it helps to use an actual photo of your pet, as long as you feel able to cope with photos; sometimes, the emotions are too raw to face looking at pictures.

Once you've chosen your mental picture or photo, keep it in mind for as long as you can, allowing yourself to take in all the details and sense the feelings that go with it. Don't worry if this makes you cry; just let the tears flow, but keep focusing on the positivity of the scene in your mind.

Have this as your "go to" mental image, or you could think about it as your new "mental screensaver". Next time the distressing image flits into your mind, try to concentrate on swiping your new "mental screen saver" over the negative picture. Initially, it will be difficult, and you may not manage it, but keep trying, gently calling to mind the positive picture. If it helps, take slow and steady deep breaths at the same time.

Over time, with consistent effort and focus, you may find that you're able to overwrite the distressing scene with a happier snapshot of your pet's life.

If you continue to struggle with flashbacks of the traumatic incident, suffer nightmares, or generally feel unable to cope, do not hesitate to seek help from a suitable professional.

PART FOUR

········

Self-Care throughout Pet Loss

17

Taking Care of Yourself during the Grief Process

Although this has been touched on in previous chapters, it's certainly worth focusing on your own wellbeing in more detail. You may have invested a lot of time and care in ensuring that your pet was as comfortable as possible leading up to the close of their time, and perhaps you're now trying to carry on with life and keep things as normal as possible for yourself and maybe your family.

As you may realize, emotions have a strong impact on wellbeing, so it makes good sense to take extra care of yourself during this time.

There is no doubt that grief can be exhausting, draining, and make one feel generally run down, so that coping with everyday things, such as work and looking after the home, becomes much more of a struggle than it would be normally.

> **Special Considerations about Personal Medical Conditions and Health Issues**
> Physical and mental health issues, such as diabetes, heart conditions, depression, and asthma, can be affected by shock and emotional upset. If you are affected, do not hesitate to seek advice from your healthcare professionals during this turbulent time.

Sleeping

It is common to find it difficult to sleep for a few nights following a significant loss. If you experience this, avoid stimulants such as caffeine or alcohol for several hours before bedtime, and it may be worth trying some natural sleep remedies. If you can, plan your days with activities that won't be stressful or need strong mental focus, such as driving long distances. If you're still suffering from insomnia after three or four nights, you may need to consult your doctor or therapist for further help.

Eating

Shock can affect the appetite, and you may find that you're not really hungry, perhaps even feeling nauseated or sick. Try to avoid just filling up on biscuits or crisps, and plan to have at least one light, healthy, and nutritious meal each day so that you're not missing out on important food types for too long.

It's not unusual to have an upset stomach, but obviously if this persists or your appetite doesn't return after a few days, do go and see your doctor to check whether everything is okay.

Staying Hydrated

It is easy to become dehydrated during grief because the body loses fluids from tears and from not feeling like eating or drinking much. Dehydration can cause various unpleasant symptoms such as:

- dry mouth
- headaches
- dizziness
- fatigue
- generally feeling unwell

It can even cause mental confusion. Although you may not actually feel thirsty, your body could be crying out for fluids, so set yourself a programme of having a glass of water or juice or a hot drink every hour during the daytime.

It's wise to limit the amount of alcohol because it can be dehydrating, and too much caffeine can make you feel jittery.

Your General Health

It's important to recognize that you are going through a significant process and need to consider how to maintain your own health and wellbeing. Rather than taking a random approach, have a think about what will help you through this immensely difficult period.

For example, you could look at the best way to reintegrate into everyday life, including work situations or regular social activities. Are you the kind of person who copes better by having some quiet time each day, avoiding pressured or stressful situations? Or do you prefer to go out and see other people to help you to take your mind off things?

One lady who worked in a doctors' surgery told me that she went straight back into work after she lost her dog. She did phone someone beforehand to say what had happened and to ask her colleagues not to say anything. She was aware that some people were sympathetic, whilst others didn't really understand the immense upset one can feel after losing such a beloved companion animal. She said she was able to throw herself into her work and felt a bit removed from her pain while she was there, but would cry throughout the drive home and found going into an empty house incredibly difficult.

Another lady explained how she needed to take time out of work after she lost her dog, and how she coped when she went back into the office:

> *Thankfully, everyone at work knew how much I love animals, and understood that my dog meant the absolute world to me, so when Lily died on the weekend, I felt confident that I could contact my manager, Lynne, to ask to take a few days of my annual leave entitlement. I was too distraught to phone in, so I emailed to explain what had happened. It was a relief when Lynne promptly emailed me back to say to take what time I needed. This gave me the much-needed space to work through that awful initial feeling of shock and then the tears—I couldn't stop crying for ages. I needed time to take on board what had happened and to get through the worst of it while everything felt so incredibly raw. After a few days, I emailed to say that I would be returning to work but asked that no one say anything to me about losing Lily, because I knew that the mention of her name would be enough to make me break down into tears, which I didn't want to do in the office.*
>
> *My colleagues were brilliant, and no one mentioned Lily for about a week, when a friend said she needed to say how sorry she was to hear my sad news. By that time, I could just about cope with the conversation.*

These two examples demonstrate that it can be really useful to give some thought as to how best to reintegrate into your normal daily activities, rather than ploughing back in without any forethought. For example, you may need to return straight to work but not wish to discuss what has happened with colleagues, either because you don't think they would understand or so that you don't break down in tears. It can sometimes be better to simply keep yourself to yourself and if anyone asks if you're okay, say that you're not feeling too well. It's about doing whatever you need to watch your own back while you're struggling with the initial stage of raw grief.

In summary, it is important to understand that grief is a process that we all have to work through from time to time in our lives. It takes time and effort and can be exhausting and draining; therefore, you need to look after yourself both physically and emotionally, especially in the early stages when you may feel particularly vulnerable.

The following relaxation exercise is designed to allow you to gently release some of the stress and strain which may have built up in your body.

ACTIVITY: Relaxation Exercise

- Lie down and support your head with a pillow.
- Take a couple of deep but gentle breaths, and allow what is currently on your mind to gently slip to one side.
- Become aware of your head resting on the pillow. Gradually, let your head sink further into the pillow. Feel the pillow supporting your head, taking the strain and allowing you to rest your head fully.
- Your shoulders are starting to relax and release into the surface beneath you. Take a deep breath into your chest, and as you exhale allow any stored tension to release.
- Become aware of your back. Feel the surface beneath you willingly taking the weight of your back. Your back is fully supported and can let go of any tension that it has been holding. Feel your back and the surface beneath it becoming one.
- Take a moment to notice the rhythm of your breath, its slow steady pace, as a feeling of calmness washes over you.
- Continue to breathe gently and slowly.

- Take a slow deep breath in, allowing the air to fill your chest and then your stomach. Exhale slowly, releasing any tension you may have been holding in the stomach. Repeat once more.

- Continue to breathe gently and slowly.

- Become aware of your legs. Feel the powerful muscles of your thighs. Gradually, allow them to rest, and use your out-breath to allow the rest to deepen. Your knees too will begin to soften as they release any tightness. Allow this feeling of relaxation to spread down through your calf muscles and into your feet.

- On your next inhalation, take a long slow breath and allow the air to travel into your chest, through your stomach, and down your legs to the tips of your toes. Exhale slowly, allowing any remaining tension to flow out of your body.

- Remain fully relaxed for as long as you feel comfortable. Slowly stretch the muscles in your legs and arms before continuing with your day.

18

When to Seek Professional Help

While it is normal to feel intense emotional turmoil in grief, there are times when professional support is needed.

People who suffer from depression can be particularly vulnerable, as can those who suffer anxiety in their everyday lives, and may find it becomes overwhelming during grief.

As has been mentioned in other sections of this book, do not hesitate to seek professional help if you are struggling to cope with the loss of your pet, whether it be physical, mental, behavioural, or emotional aspects, such as:

- Continuing and unusual insomnia
- Continuing loss of appetite
- Drinking more alcohol
- Turning to illegal substances
- Not taking care of yourself as you would normally
- Feeling aggressive towards others
- Depression that never lifts
- Constant anger
- Not being able to cope with daily life
- Constant anxiety
- Feeling worthless
- Feeling there is no hope
- Suicidal thoughts and feelings

Suicidal Thoughts
People often remark that they don't know how they'll cope without their loved one, and this can be the case whether the loss is of a person or pet. However, thoughts about "going to join" the deceased must be taken seriously. Thinking about taking one's own life, perhaps even visualizing how this would be done, is not a normal part of the grieving process. If you experience such thoughts, please seek support without delay.

Perhaps you have a friend or relative in whom you can confide initially and who could support you in getting the help you need. If you don't feel there is anyone in particular you can turn to at the time, take a look at the list of suggestions below.

Understandably, it can be difficult to start such a conversation, but often the best way is to simply and honestly explain how you are feeling, and what you are thinking. You could start by saying something such as "I can't cope". Or you could write down your thoughts and show these to the person you want to talk to.

The main point about this is that if you are in any doubt about your ability to cope, seek help immediately. Do not worry about what you say sounds like, or feel you are bothering or upsetting others, because there are people who recognize that your feelings count as much as anyone else's, and who would want to help.

When Grief Becomes Complicated

Sometimes a loss can trigger grief from previous bereavements that were never fully resolved at the time or occur soon after one another. The new loss may come on the back of other losses or stressful events, such as a partnership breakup, losing one's job, or having to relocate, or there may be other background issues that make it particularly difficult to work through the grief. If you do not feel as though you are coping, and constantly feel low, tearful, and unable to cope with aspects of everyday life, find out what professional support is available to help you get through this distressing time.

Where to Get Professional Help

Depending on the circumstances, there are different options for professional help. Some are free, whilst others will incur a fee:

- For urgent medical help or advice in the UK, visit NHS 111 online, or dial 111 for the NHS helpline. For life-threatening emergency, dial 999, or go to your nearest hospital Accident & Emergency (A&E) department.
- In the US, dial 911 for emergency
- Organizations that help with crisis (for example, the Samaritans)
- General practitioner
- Mental health practitioner
- Mental health support organization

- Pet bereavement counsellor
- Pet bereavement support organization
- General counsellor who specializes in bereavement support
- See also Resources at the end of the book.

Remember that grief can be incredibly difficult to cope with, and sometimes we need support and help. This is the case whether the grief is from losing a person or a companion animal.

19

Setbacks and Preparing for Poignant Dates and Anniversaries

As time progresses, and as the rawness of the initial shock and distress subsides, hopefully you will begin to feel more settled in your mind and heart about your loss. But it helps to be aware that certain things in daily life can suddenly trigger your emotions, causing floods of tears and/or feeling low. It can seem as if you're right back at square one, but it's most likely that you're having a temporary setback.

As previously described, the process can be like taking three steps forward and feeling good, then having to take two steps back, or three steps forward and one step back. Realize that despite these backwards movements, you are actually making progress.

Setbacks can occur soon after a loss or even a year or two later, when something seemingly small links you to a poignant memory and the emotions you felt at that time. Here are a couple of examples:

Just one bizarre moment hit me in the week, when my daughter gave the dogs some treats and took them down the garden. It reminded me of giving Bessie her last treats before taking her to the vet's to be put to sleep. I almost broke down but told my wife how I felt, and this was the first time I felt able to talk about it with her. It'll never leave me, but I feel I'm now divulging my feelings more openly.

Having asked my friend how she was coping after the recent death of her beloved collie, she told me about an unexpected setback she had experienced that morning:

I had the radio on while I was working and heard a lovely piece of music, which somehow touched a deep place in me. Suddenly, my mind went right back to being there on the living room floor, gently humming to Gracie as she was put to sleep. She had loved a particular tune since she was young, and so I'd wanted her to hear that as she slipped away, although my throat was so constricted by my emotions at the time, it was really difficult to hum it to her.

Hearing those beautiful notes on the radio took me back to that point of having to say goodbye to our lovely girl, and I found myself in floods of tears. Thankfully, the moment didn't last too long, but it took me by surprise as it came out of the blue.

Often the best way to cope is to recognize and acknowledge that you're experiencing a setback, accept that it is happening, and know that it will pass.

During bereavement, besides the unexpected triggers and setbacks, people often dread certain significant dates they have to face without their loved one. It can be especially poignant during the first year following a loss. This could be the first anniversary of the day they died, or having to get through what would normally be a happy occasion, such as a birthday or holiday, with Christmas often being a particularly difficult time.

To prepare for any such upcoming events, have a think about what you can do on that particular day. Create a plan to help you through what could otherwise be an upsetting time. You may find that doing something completely different helps, or going somewhere that you've never been before will get you through it. Or you may consciously choose to have some quiet time and be with your own thoughts and feelings, so you close the doors, switch your phone off, and spend time with your memories.

On such occasions people sometimes like to plan a little memorial for the one they loved and lost. The important thing is to do what you choose and in a way that feels right for you.

PART FIVE

· · · · · · ·

Other Aspects of Pet Loss

20

Children and Pet Bereavement

If a pet is coming to the end of their life or has already died, one of the difficulties a parent or carer may face is how to talk about the cycle of life and death to the children. Generally, it is best to keep things as simple and clear as possible when talking about death and dying—to use the words "dying" or "died", rather than trying to describe death in other ways that may cause confusion. "Euthanasia" is mostly referred to as being "put to sleep", but this can cause some young children to feel anxious about going to sleep themselves.

Children may ask all kinds of questions, such as "Why does my pet have to die?" which, of course, is difficult to answer; however, natural analogy can be helpful. For example:

We all live on a planet called Earth, and there are lots of planets and stars that you can see when you look up at the night sky. Earth is a beautiful big blue ball that whizzes around the Sun. Look around and you can see that there are lots of things living here—flowers, trees, birds, animals, fish, people, and insects.

Many different things appear, grow, and live—some, like elephants and whales, for many years, and some like flowers, tiny insects, and butterflies, only for a short time. When they come to the end of their life, they die. You can see this happen with plants and flowers in a garden or park; they go back to the earth. Have you seen the dandelions as they die back? They leave lots of seeds that float through the air so that more flowers can grow another season.

Why do things die? If nothing ever died on Planet Earth it would keep filling up and filling up, and then there would be no more space left for new lives to appear. Pets die, too. Of course, it is very sad when much-loved pets die because we miss them. But while they were alive, you cared for them with kindness and gave them lots of love, which helped them to be happy.

While you don't need to give your child upsetting details about a pet's illness or the nature of their death, being honest and straightforward is considered to be the best way forward. Telling the truth engenders trust and avoids unnecessary difficulties and misunderstandings later on. It is obviously very difficult to tell a child that their much-loved pet will soon die, but it can help to explain that you don't want the pet to suffer. Similarly, if the pet has already died, it can be a comfort to know that they weren't allowed to be in pain for any length of time.

You may feel that the children, especially teenagers, should be involved in the important decision about the need for euthanasia and the timing of it, but this obviously depends on their age and maturity, and how you think they would cope. Alternatively, it may work better to make the decision and to then gently explain to the children what is going to happen, when, and why.

Saying goodbye is difficult for the whole family. If possible, offer each child a little private time to say their goodbye and to tell the pet how much they loved them. If the animal has died unexpectedly and you are worried about the children seeing any injuries or wounds, carefully cover the body leaving a part that's intact for them to see and touch if they wish.

Ceremonies and memorials are a good way for the family to gather together to say a final goodbye to a much-loved pet, whether they are being buried in the garden or otherwise. Children sometimes want to create a special place in the garden by arranging stones and bits and pieces to mark the grave or memorial site.

Some children like to put together a memory box of mementos and write poems or letters to the pet they are grieving over.

Below are some simple activities to help young children to express what they are feeling. They'll need a pen, coloured pencils, and paper.

ACTIVITY: Activities for Children

Draw some shapes, and write in words to say how you feel, like the ones below. You can colour them in as well.

How I Feel

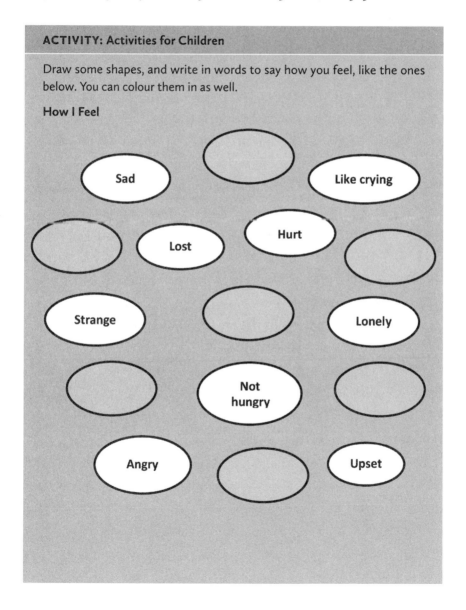

You can write a little story or poem about your pet, and say what he or she was like. Were they cuddly and soft to hold? What sort of sounds did they make? Did they make you giggle sometimes because they were funny?

You can draw more shapes and write in your own words to describe your pet, like the ones here.

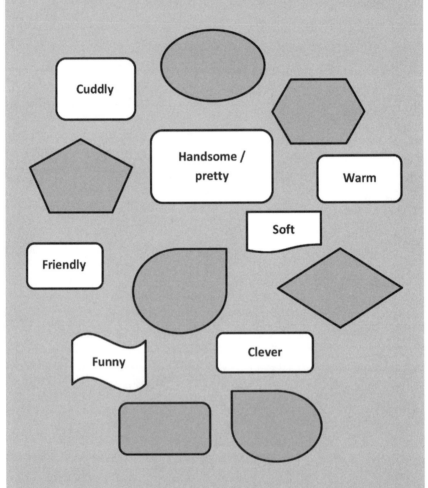

You will always have these happy things to remember about your pet.

Do you want to write your most favourite memory on a piece of paper? You can decorate it with lots of colours and shapes, and when it is finished you can keep it in a special place.

Children do not necessarily show their grief in the same way as adults, and sometimes they start to grieve some weeks after the loss, in which case you may not automatically make the association with pet bereavement. Whilst a child gives the impression that they are perfectly okay and not too upset around the time of the transition, it is important to be aware that it's possible that their grief hasn't yet found its way to the surface.

Besides crying or possibly becoming withdrawn, they may suffer nightmares, have stomachache or headaches, or be off their food. There may be problems at school, such as behaving differently in class, or their standard of work dropping. Sometimes it is worth mentioning to the class teacher what has happened so that they can be aware.

Reassure the child that it is okay to feel sad, upset, or however they may feel. Let them know that you recognize what a special relationship they had with the pet, and how they personally contributed to helping to make their life a happy one. You can give examples to back this up, such as, "You remember how you always gave Bunny a little treat and a cuddle each evening? He used to love that and would look forward to seeing you."

Whilst you may feel that you don't want to show that you yourself are upset in front of the children, grieving as a family encourages an openness and freedom to express what you're all going through together. After all, if the pet was considered a much-loved member of the family, the sense of loss will be significant, and each of you will need to work through the grief. It is always good to talk, not only about how you each feel but also to remember your pet's many special qualities and the happy times you all shared.

To conclude this chapter, here is a lovely poem written by Lauren Jepson, who was aged ten when her beautiful black hamster, Lance, died back in 2002.

Do Not Sit and Cry – You'll Only Ask Why

Do not sit and cry,
You'll only ask why.
Don't weep,
It's only my shell in deep, dark sleep.
I know you wish I were alive,
You want me to run and thrive.
Try to live normal, night and day,
It'll make us both happy in a way.
So do not sit and cry,
You'll only ask why.

21

Caring for Grieving Animals

The ongoing controversy about how animals feel and think will probably continue until such time as the human race reaches a true understanding about these other life forms with which we share this planet. In the
meantime, a conversation with fellow animal carers will soon reveal many
anecdotes about the intelligence and sensitivity seen or sensed in their
beloved charges. Whilst there is clearly much room for natural research into
this area, some of us have certainly experienced what looks like grief in a
surviving pet. This may be from the loss of another pet or the human who
previously cared for them. And sometimes, the pet's distress may be a combi-
nation of their own loss and a reaction to the general upset and fallout within
the household.

To expand a little on pet grief, I'd like to share this story about a little
dog whose guardian died suddenly and unexpectedly. It demonstrates the
animal's grief and reaction to the upset in the home:

*A few years ago I regularly stopped to chat to an elderly gentleman who
walked his Jack Russell terrier in the local park each day, where I often
took my own dog. The dog was called Ruby, as the gentleman and his
wife had taken her in on their Ruby wedding anniversary nine years
previously. Unfortunately, this gentleman suddenly became ill and died,
leaving his disabled wife and his dog grieving sorely for him.*

*Realizing that the wife was unable to walk Ruby, I offered to regu-
larly call in to pick her up and walk her with my own little terrier. The
first thing I noticed was the look in Ruby's eyes—she looked incredibly
sad and mournful and had lost her usual jaunty demeanour. I know
it's easy to put our perception of feelings on animals, but her behaviour
had completely changed and she definitely seemed depressed or low. The
situation wasn't helped by the fact that the family didn't want the elderly
lady to keep Ruby because they thought the dog was too much trouble.*

*The "trouble" was escaping and making her own way to the park
along the well-trodden path that she had walked with her beloved
guardian twice every day for over nine years. I did manage to catch*

her myself a couple of times and return her home safely, but I could tell that this was one very unsettled and unhappy little dog. On reflection, I think Ruby was affected not only by losing one of her beloved owners but also by the atmosphere in the home, where she was no longer welcome by everyone in the family.

I am happy to say that eventually she was taken into a new forever home by a kind neighbour, who cared for Ruby for the rest of her life, allowing her to regain the happiness she so deserved.

If you are looking after a bereaved pet, keep a good eye on them for any changes in the way they behave, for example:

- Showing less interest in their food
- Lethargy
- Signs of anxiety
- Being unsettled at night
- Unusually, not being able to cope on their own at home
- Pacing around the house, the garden, or their enclosure
- Searching for their companion
- Being uninterested in normal activities
- Self-mutilation or intense grooming activity
- Attention-seeking more than usual

As mentioned before, some of these could be due to the animal's sensitivity to their guardian's grief. In a multi-pet family, there will likely be some changes in behaviour as the hierarchy is re-established within the surviving animal group. You may see pets exhibiting greater freedom or being more relaxed if their relationship with the deceased pet was complex. However, when pets have been strongly bonded for any length of time it seems reasonable to consider that they may become distressed by the sudden disappearance of their friend.

The following is another story from my own experience. It goes back many years, when I looked after two beautiful cockatiels.

The cockatiel pair had strongly bonded with each other, and also with me. The male, who was called Sparky, suddenly became very ill at around the age of three, and despite intensive nursing and veterinary care he died. Primrose, his mate, wasn't left as a single bird because by this time I'd taken on a few rescue budgies. But she definitely showed signs of missing Sparky.

She would sit on my shoulder, hiding her head under my hair—something she had never done previously. After about a month I decided that I had to find her another mate, because she continued to pine. Happily, in time she accepted her new companion, and the pair bonded well.

Caring for a Bereaved Pet

Whilst it is natural for there to be a period of adjustment following the loss of a companion animal or guardian, if the bereaved pet's behaviour changes suddenly and dramatically, or does not appear to settle down after a few days, they need to be checked by a vet. This is because an underlying medical problem may coincide with the death or, as can happen with strongly bonded equines such as donkeys, the loss itself can cause sudden and life-threatening illness.

I recall an incident in which a guardian asked me about their West Highland terrier, who had suddenly become very reluctant to go on his walks following the death of the guardian's other little terrier. The lady assumed that her dog was mourning the loss of the other dog, and asked if there was anything she could do to help him overcome this. Having listened to everything she told me, I strongly recommended that she take her dog to the vet, because we couldn't be sure that there wasn't something medical going on that happened to coincide with her other dog's death. A week or two later, I heard back from her and, sure enough, the vet had done a thorough check and discovered that the dog had developed arthritis, which was making it painful for him to walk. Once the dog was on medication, he was able to enjoy his walks again.

This story highlights the importance of always getting a pet checked when they begin to behave differently, rather than assuming it is due to grief or other upset.

Generally, it is a good idea to keep to the usual routine with bereaved pets, so that things remain as stable and calm as possible. Although extra care and attention can be beneficial, over-fussing may actually stress a pet, because they pick up on the subtle changes of energy and emotions in the home. In some situations, though, slight adjustments in the environment may help to lift the spirits of a depressed animal; for example, taking a dog on a different route for their walk or somewhere new. Caged pets may enjoy extra free-range time in secure circumstances, whilst extra play time or new toys may be appreciated by feline companions. With all pets, it's a prime time to consider how their environment could be enriched, perhaps with extra choices of things to do, hidden treats to find, or new places for them to hide or shelter.

It is incredibly sad when a young animal loses a parent and struggles to cope, such as in the following story that a friend related to me about a litter of kittens who lost their mother to an accident.

A friend rang me to say something terrible had happened. Their young cat, which had given birth to three kittens, had been run over and had died. Her eight-year-old son, who adored the mother cat, was at school. She did not know what to say to him. I suggested that he needed to know that the cat had been run over on the road by a car and had died, although there was no need for him to see the mangled body, which was at the vet's.

A day later, the lady rang me again and said that she had told her son and he was sad and grieving, but now there was another problem. The three kittens were going around the house calling for their mother, and she did not know what to do to settle them down.

I replied that I had seen a television programme in which someone who communicated with animals had said that we could communicate with animals via mind pictures. I suggested to my friend that she try to explain to the kittens why their mother was not there via mind pictures.

A day later, she rang me again to say that she had sat down and, taking each kitten on her lap, one at a time, had talked to them as well as using mind pictures to tell them that their mother was no longer with them. After this, the kittens settled down and no longer walked around crying out for their mother. This in turn helped her son. Being able to deal with both her son and the kittens in this way calmed everything for the family.

Preparing an Animal for Separation from Another Pet or Their Guardian

When the death of an animal in a bonded pair or group is anticipated, it may be possible to adjust their routine in advance, so that it doesn't change quite so dramatically when the sick pet is no longer there. For example, if there is a bonded pair, you could feed the healthy animal on its own, and possibly exercise or play with each separately. This would need to be done very gradually and gently to avoid upsetting either pet, with particular care being taken to make sure the sick pet doesn't become stressed.

It can be incredibly upsetting when someone with sole responsibility for a companion animal becomes terminally ill, or due to age or illness needs to go into long-term care without their pet. Planning ahead can make the transition for both the person and their animal easier and less traumatic. If they are able to arrange for their pet to be rehomed by someone they know and trust, the new guardian could gradually over time take on more and more of the pet's care. This would allow the animal to adjust more easily to the new home and routine, whilst giving the guardian much-needed peace of mind that their beloved pet's future is being secured.

Alternatively, there are organizations that may be able to help, such as the Cinnamon Trust, a national charity in the UK, supporting the elderly, the terminally ill, and their pets. Again, this needs forward planning, so early contact with the charity is vital.

Allowing Companion Animals to See the Body of Their Deceased Friend

Where possible it is considered helpful to allow surviving animals to see and sniff the body of the pet that has died. Some animals won't take much notice, but there are accounts of others who spend time nudging, crying, sniffing, and walking around the remains of their companion. Although this can be distressing to witness, it is thought that it prevents surviving animals searching relentlessly for their deceased companions.

However, there are times when you may feel it wouldn't help a pet to see the remains of the one who has died. As someone recounted to me about her two guinea pigs:

> When Jasper, the male, died, I instinctively felt that it wouldn't help Bella, his mate, to see his body, although normally I would do that. I think the fact that poor Jasper had been away from their enclosure a lot while he was under medical care meant that Bella had grown accustomed to being on her own. She didn't seem too upset when Jasper didn't return at all, and I was aware that, having been through some vet treatment and an operation, Jasper's body would have smelt very strange to her. So I simply kept her to her routine, making sure she had plenty of attention and company. It wasn't long before I found her a lovely new companion who, after a careful introduction, she took to very happily.

As always, it is a case of doing what you feel is best for your pet, listening to your instinct, and asking your vet for advice when necessary.

Safety Aspects

Animals that are pining are likely to act out of character and, therefore, may not respond as they normally would. For example, you may need to keep a cat in overnight for a few nights in case they go frantically searching the surrounding streets for their lost companion. Or, with a dog, check that their recall training remains effective before letting them off the lead, in case they suddenly bolt to look for their buddy who has just died. Also, be aware that a stressed animal can be uncharacteristically reactive and anxious, so this should be considered, especially when children or vulnerable people are handling them.

A Mare's Grief

To conclude this chapter, here is a blog I wrote that touches on equine grief I witnessed during a session of Equine Facilitated Therapy:

> Equine Facilitated Therapy (EFT) is described as an opportunity to learn more about yourself and how you communicate, with the horses reflecting how you interact with others, affect other people, and how others affect you. It all sounds good to me!
>
> There was a nervous excitement in me as I turned up at the equine centre. Ever since I had heard about EFT, I'd wanted to experience it, so here I was—ready with an open heart and open mind.
>
> I've always sensed a depth of feeling in equines—no wonder they can form such enduring bonds within their herds, but also with those who care for them. And I longed to get a bit closer in and to feel it for myself.
>
> The weather that day was awful (following days of lovely sunshine) and not conducive to spending two hours outside in a field of horses. But there was no way I was going to be put off now that the EFT day was finally here.
>
> The session started with a chat about how I was feeling, and what I hoped to gain from the session, and the obligatory health and safety check. I confessed that I'd forgotten to bring my steel-toed work boots, but my instructor told me that my wellies were just right. She explained that some of the horses are so big and heavy that if my foot

was trodden on in steel-toed boots, the metal would be crushed into my foot. Mental note to self: keep feet away from hooves!

I explained that the thing I hoped to gain from the session was a moment of deep connection with a horse; perhaps a soul connection.

I was taken through some preparatory exercises to sense what was going on in me and to slow everything down inside. Having explained about how to approach each horse quietly and with respect for their personal space, and how to read subtle changes in body language, I was let loose into the field of horses. They were all rather intent on eating, earnestly pulling at the grass or piles of hay, so they were not concerned or interested in my tentative requests to make contact. But they didn't mind me there, and I certainly sensed different emotions with the two I did approach.

The smallest horse was a young male. I felt incredibly emotional in his presence, overwhelmingly so. I found out later that he'd had a rough start in life. The other horse, a magnificent shire, gave me a totally different feeling—sort of quick and excited; he was altogether a more confident, mature horse. But from both, I got the sense that they were very happy to be living there in that special equine centre.

Eventually the rain and cold drove us inside to the stalls. Housed in here were two of the instructor's own beautiful mares. I had been drawn to them earlier, but was respectful of their need for space and privacy, as they each had a note to say they had only recently arrived at the centre and were still settling in. However, the instructor said that it was fine to greet them, as the signs were there to ensure they weren't overwhelmed by attention from visitors.

So I quietly approached one of the mares, then it all changed. I gazed softly at the black shire mare in front of me. I let her sniff my hand and gently touched her neck when I felt she was happy for me to do that. Her long, thick fringe almost covered her eyes, but I could see the gentle spirit that shone through. My instructor explained that she had been through a very difficult few months, having been grief-stricken with the sudden death of her two-month-old foal. I felt an incredible tenderness and gently stroked her.

"You can go in with her if you want," I was told. Without hesitation, I entered her stall; there we were—one small human and one beautiful and impressively huge shire mare, together in a few moments of quiet understanding and exchange. She was incredibly sturdy yet

gentle—what a warm, loving spirit. A lump formed in my throat—her grief was palpable. I sent her healing thoughts, holding my hands on her. A little later I quietly withdrew, knowing that something had passed between us.

As I walked away afterwards, I reflected on her grief, and on the depth of feelings that these beautiful "other people" have—often not recognized in our world. But today it was recognized, respected, and revered. What an honour.

22

Phenomena in Pet Bereavement

Over the years of supporting many people through pet loss I have certainly come across stories where guardians have sensed, heard, or seen their beloved companion animal after they had died. Sometimes, they might see the cat or dog out of the corner of their eye, or even feel the familiar thud of their pet jumping onto their bed at night.

An elderly friend of mine for more years than I can remember often heard the cat flap opening and closing following the loss of her much-loved and long-lived cat, Petra. And I remember a relative saying that following the death of her dear old white mongrel, Ted, she'd sometimes see something white out of the corner of her eye.

This gentleman shared his experience of seeing images of his beloved cat for many years following his pet's transition:

Our cat, Sidney, reached 17 years of age. He had lived a good life as a much-loved member of our family. After he was euthanized, which was carried out by the vet at our home, I sat with his body for about an hour and a half or maybe two hours. There was much grief felt at his passing. Later, we conducted a little ceremony, where his body was buried in the back garden.

After his passing, I frequently saw in my peripheral vision an image of Sidney sat on the floor. It happened in any room in the house, and as soon as I looked directly towards the image, it disappeared. I believe that a physical being, once departed, leaves behind a print of their life in the fabric of the place where they lived, which, like a ghost, can be seen. To this day, some 16 years later, I occasionally still see these images of Sidney.

Another guardian describes what she saw following the death of her cat:

After one of our beloved cats died, I kept on catching glimpses of a black shape on the floor and thought that it was her, but on looking at the spot, there was nothing there. This happened over a period of time after her passing. This particular cat had been mostly black with a bit of white.

A good friend, Eleanor, who has cared for and bred German shepherd dogs for over 30 years, told me of her experiences during two of her pet bereavements. She explains:

> *I was living on Dartmoor at the time. Shogun was my first German shepherd dog, and he came to me as his fourth home, his previous life having been difficult. He arrived with many health problems, which over time I tried to sort out. However, eventually it came to a point where the poor dog was suffering and I had to make the painful decision to have him put to sleep. Thankfully, I had by then taken on another two beautiful German shepherds, so I still had canine company.*
>
> *A few days after Shogun's death, looking through the kitchen window I noticed one of the dogs sitting outside, looking as though he wanted to come in. For a brief moment I assumed it was one of my two canines, but then I realized that they were both already in the house. The dog I could see through the window looked just like Shogun.*
>
> *Shortly after that, on another occasion, I was walking by a river with my two dogs, who were roaming around enjoying some freedom. Suddenly, I realized that I was in fact seeing three dogs running around together having a wonderful time. Again, the third dog looked just like Shogun, but a Shogun who was fit and able to run with the rest of the pack. It felt magical, especially as he hadn't been able to run like that for some time before his death.*
>
> *Years later, I had another similar experience. I lived in an old railway cottage in Northamptonshire, which again I shared with three beautiful German shepherd dogs. A kindly neighbour helped me out by looking after them at times, which invariably included walking them.*
>
> *The oldest dog, Jesse, had become very frail at just over 16 years—an amazing age for a large breed. When she started having epileptic fits, the vet explained that she had reached the end of her life because her kidneys were shutting down and toxins were loading into her brain and body. Clearly, it was time to say goodbye to this dear old canine friend, so I arranged for Jesse to be put to sleep at home in the cottage.*
>
> *A few days after Jesse's passing, I was driving home through the twisting country roads and turned a corner to see my neighbour walking*

my dogs; I saw that he was walking three dogs. But, of course, since Jesse's death I only had two. Amazingly, they all looked completely normal, and each dog looked in good health, including the third dog, the image of Jesse.

Each such encounter felt pretty awesome and gave me a sort of chill down my spine, but in a good way. It also left me with a great sense of settlement and the ongoing surety of life, together with the feeling that we really only understand the great cycles of life and death in a very minimal way.

As I continued to ask people about this kind of phenomenon, more and more stories have been kindly shared, such as this one about a feline companion called Tom:

My lovely black cat, Tom, who turned out to be a female, passed away at the ripe old age of 21 years. Tom had had a lucky escape as a young cat, when she was hit by a car. She dragged herself to a neighbour's house and just cried and cried until they finally came out to see what the noise was. A trip to the vet, medication, and a leg in plaster was all they could do, but they told us it was unlikely she would survive . . . well, they got that wrong!

I spent nights with her and refused to believe she would not make it. She hardly ate for days, but would take food from me. We formed a bond that lasted up to and beyond her life with us here on Earth. Parting was very hard, and a conscious effort had to be made each day not to focus on the loss of her but rather on all the lovely cuddles, purring, and antics, including getting stuck on top of a cupboard.

Then one morning while having breakfast and probably not actually thinking about her at the time, I looked out of our kitchen window and saw her sitting on top of her favourite gatepost. She was shiny and gleaming in the early morning sunshine. I held her gaze for a few seconds, but knew as soon as I blinked she would be gone, and she was. The feeling of elation inside me was immense; she had come to say she was fine, and also to say thank you for the love we had shared.

Tom made several more appearances, always in favourite spots in the garden. Our new cats would also see her sitting on the stairs in our house. At first, they were wary, but once we explained who it was, they would purr when they saw her, always on the same stair.

And here's another fascinating story about a dog called Tippy:

Our beautiful, fun, but very nervous dog, Tippy, a tri-colour collie, had a bad start in life with a young family that tormented him. He came to us at 18 months old, and the road to acceptance of us and our way of life was long. He showed his disgust at being left alone for a few hours by eating through a telephone cable in the house—a line which had only recently been connected. He also ate an entire large box of chocolates that were left to thank my parents for popping in to see him on another occasion, when we had to leave him for a morning. He also ate the paper they were wrapped in to remove any trace of them ever having been there!

He gradually adjusted and became a well-mannered if still slightly nervous dog.

He passed away aged 16 and three quarters, and it broke our hearts.

Years and years later, I was in an audience where a man was talking about pets and the afterlife. He gradually went around the room iden-tifying animal spirits that had stepped forward to be made known to their owners. There were cats, dogs, a horse, a snake, and even a cow. The man told each person the tiniest of details about the animals.

Just as he was finishing, he said, "Has anyone not had a visit?" I put my hand up. He stood for a moment and was about to say that not all pets want to step forward, when his legs shot forward like he had been pushed, and he looked up and said, "I have a collie dog here, tri-colour, white paws, and very eager to get to you. He wants you to know he is happy and had a happy life with you. He is very determined; he wasn't supposed to slip through like that by my legs. He was called Tippy because of his distinctive white paws."

I felt so elated to get the confirmation from someone else that our pets do remain in contact with us. I was of course in no way surprised that he found a way to come through that wasn't quite allowed!

Sometimes, we may see unexplained behaviour in our pets following the death of a companion, as seen in this short report:

I saw the vet and nurse arrive promptly that afternoon, as arranged by my good friend who lives next door. By this time, I'd regained my own inner calm after the earlier shock of learning that Gracie, their elderly collie, had to be put to sleep. I knew what a wrench it would be for my friend and her family, and indeed, felt my own deep sadness at the impending loss of such a delightful canine soul.

From within my own four walls, I quietly prayed that Gracie's last moments would be peaceful. The vet team left 15 minutes later, so I assumed all had gone well. At this point, my own dog became agitated, crying and unable to settle. This worried me, in case by some quirk of fate he also had become unwell, but I did wonder if his distress was due to an instinct of what had happened to Gracie.

Gracie had been his one remaining canine friend from his puppy-hood. Over the years, they'd companionably walked together, run around fields, and greeted one another politely whenever they met, either outside our front doors or out on walks. And on occasions, Gracie had come into our house, when our dog had put aside his usual territorial behaviour and acquiesced to her presence.

Wishing I could "speak dog" for real, I let him know that Gracie had "returned to the earth", and after 10 minutes, he gradually settled down before curling up and going to sleep.

There are things in life we have not yet come to fully understand, and perhaps this kind of phenomenon is one of them. But generally those who have seen, felt, or heard their pet after its transition seem comforted by the possibility that they, or perhaps their energy, are still present in some unexplained but nevertheless welcome way.

If this is something you experience, you might want to simply acknowledge it and keep it as a wonder in your mind about those things we don't yet fully comprehend.

Personally, I haven't experienced such things, other than when my beloved parrot died. I felt a beautiful sense of freedom, as the bird I'd cared for over many years was finally set free. The following is the story of parrot Poppy and me.

Loving and Losing a Parrot

It was one of those strange moments in life when you find yourself compelled to do something that is totally impractical and a touch crazy.

I was at the counter in a pet shop saying, "I'll take that African grey parrot, but can you accept pre-dated cheques as I don't have the funds at the moment?"

To be honest, I wasn't sure how I'd find the funds, either. It was the mid-1980s, and I'd only gone into the shop to buy some seed and millet for my cockatiels and budgies. My home was filled with a number of little waifs and strays—budgies who'd been found in a junk shop and such like.

I had not actually intended to buy the terrified grey parrot, which was desperately trying to back into a corner of its cage and was making the most awful growling noise, but I had to do something to get it out of there. (I found out later that this growl is particular to grey parrots and is a sign of deep distress or fear.) There was only one other parrot for sale, a more steady-looking Amazon parrot, and much more expensive—hopefully, too much for the three rather rough-looking young chaps who'd been eyeing up the grey. I could see that the poor grey needed a quiet home—somewhere to heal from the obvious trauma it had experienced so far in its life—and I was terrified that the lads would buy it.

The shopkeeper gratefully accepted my pre-dated cheques, crammed the poor bird into a box, and carried the heavy cage to load into my car. No doubt, she was glad to have made the sale and to get that noisy creature out of her shop. Meanwhile, I resolved to do whatever I could to guarantee a decent future for this dear creature, whether she stayed with me or went to a good bird sanctuary. Either way, I was in it for the long haul, as parrots can easily live for over 50 years.

The bird was a Timneh grey, a sub-species of the more well-known African grey. I named her Poppy because of her burgundy tail feathers, although I wasn't sure she was female. Other than that she was a mixture of light and dark greys, with eyes that had apparently recently turned yellow, showing she was about 18 months old. She had just come out of quarantine, having been bred in Belgium and transported to the UK, although later on I would wonder whether she'd been caught in the wild. I would never know for sure.

I'd been told that I would need a pair of heavy leather or sheepskin gloves to avoid being bitten by her rather daunting beak. However, first sight of my thick gloves made Poppy throw herself to floor of the cage, growling in fear. So the gloves were put away forever; this bird needed to experience gentleness, kindness, compassion, and sensitivity from someone with a decent knowledge of the species and their needs.

The first couple of years together were challenging, but in time, Poppy became a confident and happy, albeit noisy, member of the family. She liked her freedom and would spend most of the time on top of her cage, as she felt safe higher up, from where she could fly around the room when she wanted or watch the neighbours out the window, mimicking the local birdlife and other daily sounds, such as the fax machine, lorry reversing warnings, and the piercing barking of two Jack Russell dogs who lived a couple of doors away. (Unfortunately she mimicked that racket for years and years!)

But it was lovely when she started to talk—a real treat, in fact—and sometimes, she'd respond to a question appropriately, such as when I asked, "Poppy, are you going in for your tea?" and she'd say, "Yes" and go into her cage to her food bowl! She learnt to nip me, then cry "Ow!" and say "Poppy" in an admonishing tone. She was a real character.

Unfortunately, she terrorized the other smaller birds, so I had to move her into a separate room to enable all avian family members to enjoy some freedom within the home. I discovered that she enjoyed sharing her space with small furry animals, and she struck up an endearing friendship with my pet dwarf rabbit, Hopkin, or as Poppy soon came to call him, "Little Bunny."

Their room was set up so that they could both have their cage doors open and come and go as they liked safely. Sometimes, I'd find them on the chair together, with the rabbit on the seat cushion and Poppy on the arm of the chair, chewing one of her treats. It took me a while to work out why there were grooves in the rabbit's leftover carrot when I cleaned them out at night. Eventually, I caught Poppy in the act—she was going into Hopkin's cage, even while he was there, and helping herself to his carrot! I managed to capture this on camera one day.

In later years she happily shared "her" room with two guinea pigs, but she always called them "Little Bunny", too.

She learnt to accept my husband. He always felt that he was tolerated rather than loved, but nevertheless he became very fond of Poppy and helped with the cleaning and feeding that goes with parrot care. She took to life in our new home in Devon well and began to amuse our new neighbours in the street—although she confused the elderly lady next door, who thought we were banging nails in the wall to put up pictures at odd times of the day and night. It was, in fact, Poppy tapping on the wall!

Over our 25 years together we became firm friends, and she'd love to be held or put her head down for me to gently scratch her. She was often to be found on my shoulder, and she'd nudge her head into my mug of tea to have a few sips, or bite holes in my jumper—I lost a lot of tops that way.

Parrots are very intelligent beings, and we had to stay one step ahead in finding safe chew toys to keep her and her beak busy. Even so, holes would appear in the plaster of the wall by the window sill where she'd been perching, or chunks would be taken out of the rubber seal of the double-glazed windows. If she didn't like something we'd soon know, as it was sent flying across the room—such refreshing honesty!

I'd always thought that Poppy and I would become old ladies together, and in case I died before her, I'd made provisions for her care. So it was with deep shock that I discovered her to be suddenly unwell one day. Thankfully we promptly found a vet who could do a home visit so as not to stress her. It turned out that she had a chest infection, so our daily routine became trying to get her to take antibiotics in the fruit juice she liked to sip.

Sadly, just as we thought she was getting better, she went downhill and had to be hospitalized. We went to see her in the vet hospital, where she was receiving excellent care. They told us how much she perked up when we went in, but it soon became clear that the kindest thing was to allow her to be put to sleep, which of course we agreed to do.

Over our years together, I'd longed to let Poppy go free, but, of course I never could, because she would surely die out in the wild. It helped with the deep sadness at losing such a wonderful companion to know that at last my dear Poppy could go free. Now she'd fly off to wherever birds go at the end of their time, leaving behind sweet memories of a most wonderful human-avian relationship. Of course, losing a pet after so many years together was immensely sad, and she is still missed today, but I feel honoured and enriched at having shared 25 years with the beautiful, funny, and confident little person Poppy became.

Raja: Part Two

To conclude this chapter on phenomena, we'll take up the final part of Hildreth Grace's poignant story about Raja, her beloved cat (which started in Chapter 12):

> We buried Raja at the edge of a forest behind the house, with a favourite cat toy to wish him joy in his next cat life. And this is the thing: I believe in reincarnation. The only tangible proof that I have is the seasons—winter becomes spring and so on. I simply feel that it makes sense. Nature is very efficient and doesn't waste anything.
>
> So I made a deal with Raja before he left. I told him that if he wanted to live with us again in his next life, that we would welcome him. I reminded him of his loud meow when he was a kitten, and told him that

is how I'd know it was him. I told him about our friend, Nicoal, down the road who fosters kittens for the Humane Society, and that was one way he could find his way back to us if he needed to.

I never felt moved to visit Raja's grave until about three and a half months later. I was out working on the horse fence one evening, when I was suddenly compelled to go over to his grave. As I was walking towards it, a brief feeling of glee overcame me and with the translation, "He's in a kitten body."

Once there, I sent him love and strength, wherever he was, feeling that heart connection still alive as my hands pulsed with healing energy. I reminded him about the guidelines for finding us if he wanted to.

That night I got an email from Nicoal, who had just brought home two black, long-haired kittens! So, next day, off we go to meet possible Raja. This was completely new territory for me.

When I walked in and saw the two kittens (a brother and a sister) in their kitten tree, I said, "He's the one on the left!" He looked at me and let out a meow! We spent the rest of the visit giving him tests, and he simply wanted to be with me the entire time, even attaching himself to my neck the way I used to carry Raja, draped over my shoulder. Two more visits and three weeks later, and now called Pluto Arjuna Raju (Juna), we brought him home to join his family. He passed every test, and I could not risk going back on my word.

We can never know for sure if this is the reincarnation of Raja. My heart believes it to be so, and there is plenty of evidence to support it. Whatever the case, one thing remains infallible: these furry beings who share their lives with us humans carry the keys to unlocking, healing, and infinitely expanding our hearts.

I hope this story may bring comfort and easement to others whose heart threads have been stretched into the unknown. May we do all that we can to grow the value, respect, and care now needed by every species across the globe, and return the favour with hearts of abundant gladness and gratitude.

23

Reflecting on the Qualities
of Your Pet

As the turmoil of your loss gradually begins to settle, bringing much-needed moments of calm, you may wish to reflect on the very special and unique qualities you valued throughout your beloved pet's life.

You may feel drawn to write a few lines, even a poem, or to lodge your thoughts on one of the pet bereavement memorial websites to be found on the internet. Or it may feel more natural to simply know it in your heart and mind. Either way, taking the time to think about your companion animal's particular qualities can facilitate the gentle healing the grief process offers. One couple share how they remembered their much-loved cat called Star:

Our beloved cat Star, aged 17 years, died of feline leukaemia, which did not appear until the last few months of her life, resulting in a large tumour growing inside her intestines, causing sudden weight loss and pain. From the moment she joined us, she became part of our family, and when the time came to have the vet put her to sleep, we decided we wanted it to take place in her own home. Yes, a visit to the surgery would have been a lot less expensive, but she was not a cat who travelled well in cars and the journey would have been stressful and uncomfortable, whereas we felt this was a way of easing the passage of her death by it taking place in a familiar place of settlement and love. As for our own easement, the following helped a lot:

- *We told her it was her time to go, and her last few hours were spent with us.*
- *We held her when she passed away and felt her last breath.*
- *We buried her in our garden in one of her favourite places.*
- *We thought about her life and her special ways and wrote single-word descriptions on 17 stones as dedications to surround her grave.*

We wrote the following poem as a tribute to her life:

To Star, Our Nearby Friend

Long will we remember you,
Dear companion of our days.
For many years you graced us,
With your presence and endearing ways.
Among your kind you were special to us,
Giving so freely your loyalty and trust.
For all life there comes a time to die,
But in our hearts, you are always nearby.

I am grateful to Liz Ive for sharing her thoughts and reflections on losing Star, and for the little gems she shared about what helped her and her husband during their bereavement.

Over the years I have certainly found it helpful to reflect and write about the many little creatures that I have loved and lost. This is a poem written way back in 1988, after my first pet bird, Sparky, died:

A Cockatiel Called Sparky

Called Sparky, for the spark in the eye,
And the questioning look that seemed to ask, "Why?"
Protective of Primrose, his mate in abode,
He ruled the roost and set the code.
Greeting us with squawks as we came home,
With Sparky around, you never felt alone.

Whistling tunes we heard many a time,
Starting him off, he would finish the rhyme.
Probably the noisiest bird we had here,
Brave and inquisitive, he rarely showed fear.
Sadly you're missed, little bird, now you've gone,
In this world, it appeared, you weren't to dwell long.
I want to remember the good times we had,
In fact, I remember none of them were bad.
You were always full of yourself, which is right,
You were a bird of fun, sharing, and delight.
Friendly, and firmly part of our lives,
With Primrose, who aptly was called your wife.
Now she sits with me, missing you, no doubt,
As she looks here and there and roundabout.
However, the times we all spent together so well,
As friends on this planet, where we dwell,
Were times not to be forgotten, but remembered with gladness,
Stronger and firmer than this sudden sadness.
In my heart I need to say "Thank you" to you . . .
For being what you were . . . a cockatiel through and through.

This moving poem was written by a vet about her wonderful black Labrador, who was a treasured friend from the day he joined her family on 21 January 2005 until he left this world on 17 August 2016, with his head resting on her knee, in the sunshine, surrounded by the people who loved him dearly in this life.

Frisby – Treasured Friend

A shoulder to cry on, a soft ear to bend.
Unconditional love from my Labrador friend.
Keeper of secrets and disastrous tales.
Late night protection from amorous males.
Running mate, partner, and chewer of shoes.
Producer of the most inappropriate poos.
Stealer of biscuits, Hoover for toast.
Frisby was the dog who was loved by us most.
Adventures with family, and singing for joy,
Pavarotti lives on in a black canine boy.
Swimming in France in his own special pool,

Polo at Cowdrey . . . that dog was no fool!
Model "patient" for children to practise their skill;
Knight, Dragon or Gruffalo, dressed up as they will.
Patient serenity at the end of his years,
and still I mourn daily for those velvety ears.
A shoulder to cry on, a soft ear to bend.
To Frisby, I love you, my most treasured friend.

To conclude this chapter, I'm honoured to share a tribute written by my close friend Mel about her lovely dog, Mia, who was known and loved by many from early, very active puppyhood through to her more sedate years of maturity.

In Tribute to – Miakoda, the Singing Utonagan,
Also known as Mia, but better known as Dippy!

On Thursday night, my return from work was met with an eerie silence . . . no singing Utonagan heralding my return home and her much-anticipated dinner.

I quickly scanned the garden—no Mia. I scanned the house—no Mia. Had she escaped again, as she used to do in her younger days, and was somewhere miles away wandering and hunting?

This time I took a better look in the garden, and there she was—in a cool and quiet corner; her life had clearly suddenly, unexpectedly, and hopefully painlessly, ended.

Dippy died as she had lived—independently, unexpectedly, outside, close to the Great Mother, and on her own terms.

When my friend and I collected her almost 12 years ago from Blackpool, the sweetest little puppy, the least wanted of the litter due to her "incorrect" markings, she "sang" all the way home, six very long hours. A sign of what was to come . . .

She grew up into a beautiful and independent girl—fearless, strong, and so very fast and fleet when hunting. She and her litter sister, Imana, the companion dog of my friend Sarah, shared many canine adventures together—escaping, wandering, playing, and generally getting into trouble.

Through the many trials and tribulations that naturally accompany a large, strong dog coming of age, Mia was a challenge, and allowed me to exercise and grow patience, tolerance, and ingenuity in offering her some degree of freedom balanced with safety and control. Life with Dippy was certainly never boring!

She is now resting along with her canine companions Shimba and Meg, three old ladies together. Her presence will be sorely missed, but her life was long, healthy, and happy, and she was loved.

Run free, dear Dip, finally liberated from the restrictions of age, arthritis, and human control!

24

Opening Your Heart and Home to Another Pet

I avidly read James Herriot's books years ago, including his biography, and I seem to recall that he suggested to anyone grieving over the loss of their dog that it would help them to get another one soon. Today, this isn't the advice that is given out, although it may work for some people. An acquaintance told me that when she lost her golden retriever some years back, she was on the phone to a retriever rescue organization within a couple of days, as she couldn't bear to be without a dog. It worked well for her, but it's certainly not the way to go for everyone.

Taking on another pet too soon may sometimes create a difficulty in bonding, which can be unfair on the new animal, which is trying to adapt to a new circumstance. A bereaved person who came to me for support was struggling to accept her new dog after the loss of a very special one. During our conversation it became clear that, on reflection, she hadn't really felt ready to take on the new canine friend and, subsequently, it was difficult for her to bond. I believe she did in the end, but it created a rather bumpy start to their relationship.

Sometimes, however, things just seem to happen, and a new animal seems to land in your lap, as shown in my own story about a new puppy.

After losing our deeply loved Bobby, a three-legged terrier we rehomed from the RSPCA Dogs Home in Bristol, my husband and I were totally devastated. When, by chance, we heard about a puppy needing a new home, it somehow felt like fate was throwing us a lifeline. Feeling the desperate need for canine company and a strong instinct that we were meant to give this little dog a new home, we agreed to meet him.

The gorgeous puppy melted our hearts immediately—he was here to stay, although I confess that I'd already made my mind up before even meeting him!

There were difficulties and struggles initially, as is often the case, but this little chap was smart and learnt quickly. However, I do remember that during those early days together, I felt almost guilty and worried that my love for him didn't run as deep as it had done for Bobby. It was when I took him to meet two of my dearest friends that this changed. One of them remarked that she could see how much we loved each other already. Somehow hearing this from someone else really helped me, and since then I've never looked back.

Giving Yourself Time

There is no doubt that the death of a pet leaves a big hole in your life, which you may feel must be filled as soon as possible, like the person who desperately needed another golden retriever. However, let's look at things to consider when making such an important decision.

As detailed earlier, the shock of bereavement often causes confusion and emotional turmoil, so it's not an ideal time to make a life-changing decision. Allow yourself space to work through your grief, so that you can be sure that you're not simply trying to make the pain go away by taking on another pet. Getting a new pet may help to ease your journey through grief, but if the timing isn't right, or if you choose an animal purely on a reactionary basis, it could cause problems for you and, of course, for the new pet. You need to be as sure as you can so try not to rush into anything.

A Family Decision

Everyone in the family may not agree about what to do. Someone may say, "That's it—never again!" because they feel that they simply couldn't face ever loving and losing another pet for the rest of their life, as their current grief is so profoundly overwhelming. Obviously, this is difficult when other family members are desperate for another pet to love. Again, allow time for everyone to work through their grief before trying to make a collective decision.

Other Family Pets

There may be other pets to consider. Elderly animals may not take well to a youngster invading their territory, and survivors of a bonded group or pair could react badly if a new pet is introduced too quickly or without careful planning.

Knowing what to do, and when, is often a fine balancing act, as can be seen in my own story, which thankfully had a happy conclusion.

Sparky, my first beautiful cockatiel, became suddenly ill, and despite prompt veterinary treatment he died. I was heart-broken at losing such an amazing little character.

Primrose, his mate, of whom he had been highly protective, also seemed devastated. She'd perch on my shoulder, as she often did, but now with her head buried under my hair, as if she was trying to hide. It was heart-breaking, and it didn't feel right to keep such a sociable species of bird without a mate, so I set out to find her another male of a similar age.

Primrose became very excited when she heard the distinctive call of a cockatiel coming from the pet carrier as I brought the new, carefully chosen bird into the house. However, when she realized that it wasn't Sparky but a newcomer, she became alarmingly agitated, flying and pecking at the poor scared creature, who cowered in the carrier. At this point, I was worried about whether I had done the right thing, but my gut feeling told me that it would work out in time.

As it was, I had to keep them housed apart for a while to avoid transferring any underlying disease from the new bird, but I allowed them to see and hear each other from a safe distance.

By the time it was safe to let them both free in their room to meet properly they'd become more accustomed to the sight and sound of each other and thankfully it wasn't too long before they became a strongly bonded pair.

If you're unsure whether to offer a new pet a forever home consider things, such as:

* Do you need a break from the responsibility of caring for a pet?
* Do you currently need more time for other things in life?

- Have your circumstances changed, making it more difficult to look after an animal?
- Can you afford to care for a pet at present?
- Would you like to travel and take holidays you haven't been able to do for some time?
- Do you feel concerned about the long-term security you can offer a new pet?

When my parrot, Poppy, died in 2013, my husband wondered if I wanted to take on another rescue bird. I realized, however, that I wasn't getting any younger, and parrots can live an incredibly long time. Somehow, I knew in my heart and mind that, after 30 or so years of caring for birds, it was the end of an era.

Naturally, I was shocked at her fairly sudden death and really missed my wonderful feathered friend, who'd been part of my life for so many years. It also took a while to adjust to being a non-bird household. As anyone who cares for birds will know, there is a lot of cleaning to do, and you need to dedicate much time and effort to keeping your avian friends safe, happy, and healthy. Much to my own surprise, I found that no longer having to do all this each day brought me spare time, which I eventually came to enjoy.

If you decide not to have another pet for the time being, don't be surprised at how much you miss the warmth and companionship. I must admit that after the loss of my parrot, I took every opportunity to spend time with my friend's two parrots and found myself nostalgically viewing all her avian entries on Facebook. To this day when my friend and I meet up for a chat, I still love hearing about their latest antics. However, despite missing my own avian companion, deep down I know that my decision was the right one.

I remember coming across someone else who, after recently losing her dog, had decided that it was time to bring her pet-caring era to a close.

It was twilight, and I was returning home after a long walk with Bobby, my little black-and-white cross-breed terrier. As we walked along the pavement, an older lady came towards us with an intense look in her eyes, focused on my dog. I was used to people showing an interest in Bobby, who had a real zest for life, because they often wanted to stop me to admire him and remark on how well he got around on his three legs.

We stopped to say hello, and she was soon completely absorbed in fussing over Bobby, who happily obliged by wagging his tail and gazing at her with his shiny, bright eyes. She wanted to know all about him, how he'd lost his back leg, how old he was, where he'd come from, and so on.

We stood and talked for ages, and she explained that she'd lost her own dog just a few weeks earlier and was desperate for some canine "conversation". She told me that she'd worked with rescue dogs when she was younger and said, "When you see someone like me, you need to understand that they may have recently lost their dog and really need some doggy time."

She was obviously knowledgeable about dogs, and it came out in conversation that as well as working at a high level in animal welfare and rescue, she had shared her home with many dogs over the years. But now in her maturing years, she didn't feel it was right to take on another dog.

The encounter seemed to lift her spirits, and as Bobby and I continued on our walk I felt a renewed sense of how fortunate I was at having such a wonderful canine companion in my life. However, I haven't forgotten the depth of sadness and longing in that lady's eyes. I suspect that although she'd decided she wouldn't have another dog herself, she will have continued to have her "canine conversations" by volunteering in some capacity.

Volunteering

I do sometimes suggest volunteering to bereaved people, as it affords an opportunity to be involved in caring for animals without the responsibility of personal guardianship. Many organizations depend on the regular support of their volunteers, and it can be satisfying to give one's time in this way. There are many options, such as dog walking, fostering pets for people who are unwell or in hospital, or transporting animals to the vet if the guardians are unable to do so themselves. There may be opportunities at your local animal sanctuary, involving hands-on work, raising funds, helping at events, or becoming a board member. If you're able to commit to helping out on a regular basis, you'll no doubt be made most welcome.

Feelings of Guilt

Although there is a chapter dedicated to "Coping with Guilt" earlier in the book, it's worth a mention here, because people can feel guilty whether they decide to have another pet or not.

For example, you may decide you want another pet, but you feel it's disrespectful to the one you've lost. If this is the case, consider the love and care you have to offer, and the value of giving another companion animal the chance of a happy life that otherwise, it may never have.

If you decide not to take on another pet, try to work out why that is the best decision, so that your mind is clear. Sometimes it can be financial reasons, which are entirely valid; sometimes it's time, circumstances, age, or family commitments. It may be that you need freedom from the responsibility that caring for a pet brings, or you simply cannot face the emotional turmoil of loving and losing another beloved companion animal in the foreseeable future. Whatever the reason, remember that it's valid for you, and that is what counts.

As I said earlier, when my parrot died, I somehow knew it was better not to take on another because of the time and energy it would need, which I realized I would increasingly struggle to muster in the years to come.

Looking at Practical Issues

If you do decide to open your heart and home to a new pet, take time to think about some of the practical issues. For example, what age and type of pet will work best with your current and future lifestyle? To help you to think about this, you may want to consider the following scenario:

> Emily Brown, a widow of many years, is now in her late seventies. She's still fairly fit and loves to walk every day, although she has some arthritis that slows her down these days. In fact, her doctor has mentioned surgery for her knee at some point in the future.
>
> Sadly, she's desperately missing her Border collie, Bess, who died recently at the age of 15 years. Like all her previous collies, she'd cared for Bess right from puppyhood and had brought her up to be a well-adjusted and happy dog.
>
> Her grown-up children and grandchildren can see how lonely she is and want to buy her another Border collie puppy, which they feel sure will lift her spirits— after all, a puppy is bound to lift anyone's spirits! However, Emily last took on a puppy 15 years ago, when she herself was that much younger. She'd love another dog and, although with her knowledge and experience of dogs she knows she is capable of offering one a good home, she is aware that as she herself hits 80, she may not have the energy and fitness needed to be able to care for such a young and active breed.

Would Emily be better placed to consider an older dog—maybe a different breed that is less energetic and particularly fond of lazing around on the settee? Or perhaps she might even consider a different type of pet to accompany her through her mature years?

The friend mentioned in the opening chapter of this book is now in her late seventies. She has always been a great animal lover and has had dogs and cats throughout much of her adult life. When she sadly lost her beautiful golden retriever, she realized in all honesty that although she's currently incredibly fit and healthy for her age, she could no longer comfortably guarantee life-long care for another canine.

She told me that she may take on an older cat in need of a loving home, but in the meantime, she finds herself happily busy helping friends and neighbours with their pets. In fact, she now has to turn people away because she gets so booked up dog-sitting for people when they go away on holiday.

Her realistic and down-to-earth approach enabled her to make the best decision for her advancing years, while still enjoying plenty of canine company without the long-term commitment and responsibility.

Bonding with a New Pet

It can be challenging taking on a new pet at any time, especially when the animal has behavioural issues or they have much to learn because they are young.

It's easy to think, "Oh no, what on earth have I done?" as the full realization of responsibility hits home.

Taking on a pet shortly after a significant pet loss can be particularly daunting. After all, you were used to your previous pet's numerous endearing little ways and traits, and had an ease in communicating that meant you didn't always need to say anything; you could read their expressions and body language, and they could pick up on yours. This comfortable and familiar companionship is naturally part of what is missed when a beloved pet dies.

If you've recently taken on a new pet but are finding it difficult to bond, please remember that it takes time to build a relationship. Trust needs to be engendered, and you have to get to know each other. You may find that you're comparing them to the animal you've recently lost, or that it isn't as easy to love the new animal as you thought it would be.

My suggestion is to allow yourself and your new pet the time you both need to adjust and settle in. Take the pressure off yourself and your pet. Try to relax and just be yourself and let your new companion find their feet.

This is a crucial time for the pet, so focus on giving them the care they need, even if you don't yet feel that "special something" with them. Keep trying to see things from the animal's point of view. They need to feel comfortable and secure, but there will be much for them to get used to as they learn how to adapt to the new circumstance they find themselves in.

The love and connection will develop over time, as you get to know and trust each other. And as you continue to journey through your grief, you will find that your new companion begins to bring joy and friendship into your life. In the meantime, know that you're doing something of account by offering another animal a safe, forever home—so many are in need.

To conclude this chapter, here is a story about Mark and his family, who took on a rescue dog after the devastating loss of their beloved Border collie, Jess. Jess was clearly a very special canine companion, who brought much joy to her human family. Mark is very experienced in dog agility, and thoroughly enjoys working with his charges to bring out their natural talents and intelligence.

When Jess first arrived she had a number of phobias; for example, someone coughing, sneezing, or laughing loudly would cause her to cower on the floor, as if someone had attacked her. But when she was introduced to the agility ring, Mark could see she was a "natural", and her intelligence shone through. She soon learnt to trust Mark and would happily take commands from him and no one else.

The family also had a Welsh Border collie called Meg, and although she was only a year older, she happily adopted the newcomer as her sibling. Mark noticed how Meg seemed to bring Jess out of the stress she'd endured as a puppy by introducing her into the wonderful world of natural canine play, further strengthening the bond between the two dogs.

Sadly, Jess suffered seizures, which were upsetting for everyone, including Meg, who, clearly distressed by seeing her friend go through these, became highly protective when Jess was in seizure mode.

What followed was an incredibly difficult time. The family did all they could for Jess, but everything seemed surreal during the multiple trips to the vet hospital for tests and treatment, which was by then amounting to £180 per month.

Despite all the care and medical attention, the seizures increased. Mark described how awful it was to witness poor Jess going through six seizures a day, at which point the family knew the only option for their beloved dog was euthanasia.

When Mark first sought bereavement support, the family had already taken on another rescue dog called Max, a New Zealand huntaway. The inspiration in this story is that they welcomed Max into their home in memory of their beloved Jess, giving him a second chance in life, knowing that their new charge also came with many issues and would be a real challenge.

Since first getting in touch, Mark has reported that Max has gently but surely learnt to trust them and done increasingly well in the agility ring. The latest report showed Max coming fourth out of 66 dogs!

But Max isn't the only winner in this story. Max may never reach the heights that Jess did in agility, but for Mark and his family, having him to focus on and care for continues to help them find their way through the trail of deep grief that was left by the loss of their beloved Jess.

Towards Inner Peace
and Settlement

I hope that *When It's Time to Say Goodbye* has offered you support through your personal grief journey. Everything in the book encourages you towards a simple and quiet place of inner peace. This comes from accepting or perhaps resolving many facets of your grief, from the uncertainties that prevail during the lead-up to the inevitable death of your beloved pet to coping with the aftermath and roller coaster of emotions that invariably surrounds bereavement.

Remember that grief is the other side of caring, and you grieve because you care. Grief isn't something "to get over". It's a path with many twists and turns. It is painful, difficult, and at times brings a strong sense of feeling lost and not in control.

Grief is a process we all find ourselves in from time to time throughout our lives. It's the journey we take from the point of separation from those we love, or who we value and uphold, to a place where the mind and heart can feel settled, where we can begin to quietly reorganize and adapt to the new situation we find ourselves in.

It is not something to avoid or push aside to deal with later, because the process of grief needs its time and space in you. You may need to work through each part, piece by piece, sometimes working back through things you thought you'd already dealt with.

You may have to settle your mind about different things at the various stages of your particular journey. It's very likely that you have to be courageous in facing your deepest fears, perhaps making one of the most difficult decisions in your life.

Ultimately your grief journey may teach you that "letting go" of that which is most precious to you is perhaps the greatest gift you can offer to your animal friend and yourself.

I offer the following poem and stories as an easement and support to your life.

In Remembrance of a Beloved Pet

Thank you for being what you were to me,
It's time now to move on and go free.
Thank you for sharing your life with humankind,
I know another so special would be difficult to find.

Know that during your life you were held most dear,
And because of my care for you I shed a tear.
You will be missed for a very long time,
My pain is part of your leaving, so that is fine.

Go free now, dear little one, to where your kind go,
That you were deeply loved is for you to know.

As you progress gently but surely through grief, there is a quiet healing—difficult to see at first, but it is there. It's there in the courage to pick up each new piece of your life, and carefully place it where it fits best, so that in time a new picture is formed.

The one who has moved on will always be missed, but perhaps they remain nearby, held within memories that fortify and strengthen you on your journey ahead. In closing, here are some moving accounts from others who have travelled this road.

Loving and Losing a Beloved Pet

This young lady from Holland shares the story of her special dog TumTum, beloved friend during her teens and young adult life:

> *My mother had always loved cocker spaniels. As a child, she was never allowed a dog so she walked the neighbour's cocker spaniel. As an adult she always had dogs, but it wasn't until her forties that she decided to expand her hobby to showing and breeding them. She only ever bred a handful of litters, but I would accompany her to dog shows and stay up all night with her to help deliver a litter; and I just loved the eight weeks that the puppies were growing up in our living room. Sometimes we would keep one, but I understood and accepted that most of the puppies had to leave to go to new owners.*
>
> *Then, on 30 March 2004, Tumtum was born. He was one of a litter of seven, but instantly my favourite. We had the habit of giving*

the puppies cute, temporary names for their litter time until their new owners chose their permanent name, and Tumtum is the name of a Dutch candy and perfect for his litter name.

At their usual six-week health check, the vet discovered that Tumtum had a small heart murmur. While this does not always affect them, pedigree dogs should always be sold with a clean bill of health. Mum decided to keep him a couple weeks longer, as often the murmur will close on its own. I was delighted.

I was convinced that Tumtum would stay. Mum was not. So while she tried to keep an emotional distance (to make it less hard to say goodbye to him later), I had no such inhibitions and spent lots of time with him. As a result, we bonded and, as I predicted, he never left and would remain with the name Tumtum all his life.

He was my best friend through my late teens, always waiting for me to get home from school. I would take him out wandering, or let him sleep on my lap in front of the telly. We even had a party trick, where he would leap at me and I would catch him mid-air so he could hook his front legs over my shoulders and just rain kisses on me. While I loved them all, I'd never had such a strong bond with any of our dogs before.

When I grew older, I was home less and less often. First, I was away to study, then I got my first own place. As I worked full time, he could not live with me, but I would pick him up as often as possible to take him out for a walk. And then I left to travel for six months, which turned into a year.

When I returned from my travels I planned to move in with my parents again for a little while, and I wondered if he'd remember me and if our bond would have changed. My mum only had three dogs at this point, and I could see that although they had grown closer, Tumtum was still very much my dog. Whilst he was getting older (he was now 12 years old), he remained the playful and happy dog he always was. Apart from losing his eyesight, he still looked like a young dog. I felt guilty for having been away from home so much, but also thought we'd have lots of time left.

One weekend Tumtum wasn't feeling very well. He'd thrown up his dinner and was quiet. Not necessarily something to panic about, but he grew more subdued as the day went on, and by the next day it was clear he had tummy pains. I had to leave early to go to work.

When I came home, I immediately knew something was wrong. As I opened the door, I did not even need to look. I asked my mother where Tumtum was. She said she'd taken him to the vet's that morning, where he'd had an ultrasound of his tummy. There was nothing they could do, and the kindest thing was to put him to sleep.

That evening we drove to the forest where many of our previous dogs were buried. My siblings were there as well, as is our ritual, to help dig the hole and support Mum. Mum and I picked his spot, and when the time came to collect him from the car I carried him in my arms and said my final goodbye.

I struggled with his death for a long time. A big part of that was, I think, because I wasn't there when he passed away. I asked Mum why she didn't call me, why she didn't wait for me to get there. While he had lived with her his entire life, nobody questioned that he was "my dog". But she hadn't wanted to interrupt me at work or upset me. Still, it has always haunted me.

I would imagine that he wasn't gone. When I closed my eyes, I could still recall exactly how his coat felt, how I would stroke his face and ears, how he would feel when he slept on my lap. When I was outside, I imagined he was still walking next to me, every step of my journey.

Nearly two years after his death, an Australian friend came to stay with me for three weeks, and she told me that she had done a course on animal communication. She needed to practise, and as this was for both animals that were still here and those that passed on, I gave her a picture of my Tumtum. She wrote down the conversation she had with him for me.

Basically, she said he was a very happy, playful soul, almost puppy-like. As she tried to contact him he had to come from afar and whilst happy to talk to my friend, he was also keen to get back to me. When she asked for a specific memory to give me, he told her of one Christmas with me so happy sitting under the tree, handing out presents to everyone. He also said that he didn't mind that I was not there when he passed away, and that he saw me carry him to his grave. He also said that he understood why I had to be away so much when he was still alive, that it was part of my journey. His purpose was to be with me and make me happy, and he would continue to stay with me until I trusted enough to love again.

The idea of getting another dog did not even cross my mind for years—until last year. All of a sudden, all of the circumstances were perfect and the idea would not leave my mind. I obsessed over what type of dog, where from, and so on. I really think it was the universe telling me that it was time. I was also very emotional during this time, thinking of Tumtum a lot.

I decided on a rescue dog, as they would need me as much as I needed them, and it would be an adult black dog, as they are often the ones that don't get adopted. When I saw Remy's picture it just stuck, and I knew it would be him. It was still a long wait of three months until I finally met him. In this time, I felt like I already knew him, whilst he had no idea that I existed. Seeing him for the first time wasn't a picture-perfect moment where both of us just gazed into each other's eyes; he was bursting for a wee, anxious for his friends, and busy smelling everything and meeting everyone but me. The three-and-a-half-hour drive home was spent with me looking into the back of the car, trying to see how he was doing in his crate on the backseat. He was clearly exhausted but afraid to lie down, so he slept sitting up, leaning into the side of the crate.

Taking this journey with him has been a privilege. From the car journey, where I would softly speak and sing to him, to coming home and learning he was terrified of the linoleum floor in the kitchen so I had to move his food and water bowls, to seeing his confidence grow, to the first time he dared to ask me to play with him by gently taking my hand in his mouth. All my months of planning went straight out the window, as he refused to go into the crate I got especially for night time; he now sleeps in my bed. He has done this on many occasions, as if to say, "No, Mum, I'll show you a better way." And it always is.

I was worried about adopting a street dog from overseas after only being used to the easy-going cocker spaniels, but Remy could not be clearer in his communications if he spoke the words to me. My relationship with Remy feels very much like a partnership, with mutual respect and appreciation for each other's likes and dislikes. And the weird part is I can now no longer recall how Tumtum's coat felt, the feeling of stroking his head and ears, or how he would lie on my lap. And I think of the purpose he told my friend he had for my life, and think maybe he has fulfilled it.

Here is another heart-warming account of sharing life with canine friends:

My experience of owning a dog covers two dogs: one I have lost and one I still have.

I didn't grow up with a dog, and my first experience was with a lovely Doberman bitch called Polly that we had from an eight-week-old puppy. I wish I knew then what I know now, as I'm sure we didn't do the training as well as we could have done, but, having said that, we loved her dearly. She was a real character—you could say all mouth and no trousers. I recall her speeding across the park towards a lurcher and a Jack Russell barking to play with them, but the next minute seeing her crying and running back towards me over the crest of the hill with the lurcher chasing her.

We had a couple of health scares with her over the years that could have been quite serious. Late one evening, she started bloating up around her abdomen and was desperately trying to be sick. We rushed her to the vet, who basically had to deflate her. Not long afterwards, she started showing the same behaviour, so again we took her straight to the vet's, who couldn't initially see what was wrong. However, she trusted that we knew the signs after the last time, and within half an hour of us leaving Polly was rushed in to surgery. This time, her stomach had twisted round, and if we hadn't noticed what was happening, she surely would have died in lots of pain.

These two occasions were my first experience in life of nearly losing a dog, and the feeling was overwhelming. The love you have for them is quite shocking, and unless you have owned a dog you can never understand the intensity.

We lost Polly at just shy of 11 years old. She had started coughing, and the vet said it may have been kennel cough, so to meet her in the car park at the surgery. She quickly realized this wasn't the problem, and on examining her, established that it was an enlarged heart and Polly was suffering from congestive heart failure.

We tried some medication to help her clear the fluid from her lungs over a couple of days, but nothing improved her symptoms. The vet gave her an injection, and I asked how long I should give it to work. She basically said that we would be looking at hours and if there was no improvement to bring her back in. In hindsight, I think the injection was just saline and, because the vet knew we were sensible owners and that I had understood the underlying meaning of what she was saying, she knew I would really be taking Polly home for a couple of hours to get myself ready for the final decision.

Sure enough, later that afternoon, I knew Polly had had enough and asked my friend to call the vet for me and say it was time. Before going back to the vet's for the last time, I gave Polly a bag of human chocolate buttons—what harm was it going to do?—and she absolutely loved them.

The vet was not at all surprised to see me back at the surgery. My friend came with me, and we all sat on the floor with Polly while she had her final injection. It was the hardest thing I had ever done in my life, but I came away actually feeling proud of myself for making the decision, as it was the last thing I could do for Polly.

It was very hard on my husband, who was working away and couldn't be there with us. We talked about waiting another day until he got home, but we both decided that would just be cruel as Polly was clearly suffering. I think it was worse for him, as he came home to an empty house and hadn't had that final cuddle or a chance to say goodbye. To see a grown man sobbing is just heart-breaking.

It took a good few years until we could get another dog. Changes in jobs meant we were both out all day, but finally we were in a position to get another dog, as I was very lucky to be allowed to bring a dog to work with me. This time we rehomed rather than buying a puppy, and we have never looked back.

Murphy, the cocker spaniel, is everything I didn't think I wanted—small, white hair, and long ears, but he was there at the right time. He was nearly five when he came to live with us, and he has been part of our household for six years now. It took a while before he bonded with us, and I will never forget the first time I let him off the lead in the woods after being on a long lead for six weeks. He went tearing down the path, and I thought I had judged it wrong and it was too soon. I called him, and he stopped and looked back at me and then rang at top speed straight back, making eye contact with me. That first moment of real connection is something I will never forget.

Murphy is the love of my life, and every now and then, I think that we will only have a few more years with him, as he is 11 years old. I know that when the time is right, I will again be proud that I will make the right decision for my best friend.

Here is a moving account of loving and losing a wonderful canine companion who was by the side of this lady throughout difficult times:

My Yogi Bear

We bought Yogi at the age of nine weeks old, and what a perfect pup he was—he seemed to have been born an old man! The only other way I could describe or name him was Eeyore; he really was a huge softy. After seven years of Yogi being in the family unit, unfortunately, my husband and I divorced, leaving Yogi and I together, and we found we had an amazing and inseparable bond with each other. He never left my side, so from that point on, it was him and me. We lived together, he came to work with me each and every day, and we walked for miles.

Twelve months ago, he became lame for no apparent reason. We had numerous visits to the vet but never found the underlying reason for this lameness. Last Christmas, Yogi passed away, leaving an enormous hole in my heart. He was 12 years old, a little grey around the muzzle, but he was the most amazing dog I had ever owned, and I have owned and lost a few. As he had always come to work with me, the whole office was devastated. He was taken from me so suddenly.

It's all so hard to put into words. He really was my world. The companionship and faithfulness I had from this beautiful dog was unbelievable. I never dreamt I would have been blessed with such a close friendship with an animal.

Afterwards, coming to work and walking without him, missing the company of this wonderful dog, was like losing my right arm. I am only now able to talk of him fondly without welling up inside, though it still hurts. His ashes are still under my bed, close to me, until I find the right time to be able to put him somewhere I know he will love, close to woods or water, on one of his dream walks.

Happily, sometime later, a new little friend in the form of a golden retriever puppy, called Boris, came into her life:

After a year without my dear Yogi, who left a huge hole in my heart, I just longed not for a replacement but a new adventure with a gorgeous new companion, and already I am totally besotted!

EPILOGUE

Supporting Someone Else through Pet Bereavement

In the future, you may well come across others who are struggling with the death of a much-loved companion animal. This could be a friend or family member, or a chance meeting with someone you haven't met before. You'll recognize their pain and distress, and although it may cause you to feel upset for a while, it can be a wonderful opportunity to use your own experience to offer understanding to someone else. You may find you can do this naturally and easily, but in case it's helpful, here are some tips on supporting others in pet bereavement.

People who are grieving can feel lost and confused as they try to cope with overwhelming emotions and worries. Offering some quiet and dedicated time to talk things through can be of comfort. To do this effectively, you'll need to press the pause button on the everyday issues that are going on in your own life, even if this is for five minutes, so that you can truly listen to them.

Try not to worry about what to say or what you can do; instead, focus all your energy into listening and being in the moment. Concentrate on what they are saying in words and expressing through their body language. Look at what they need at that particular moment so you can respond in a measured way rather than be reactive to their distress.

Show respect for their particular loss and their feelings. The death of a pet doesn't always elicit the same empathy and understanding as human loss, and it is important for the bereaved person to feel safe enough to show their feelings without fear of ridicule or unspoken judgement. If you want, let them know that you've been through it yourself, and reassure them that it is perfectly natural to be so upset when mourning a much-loved companion animal.

Bereavements can cause people to feel lost and alone. Be warm and open in your approach, as this helps keep the lines of communication open and will enable them to express their emotions, if they feel like sharing these with you.

Remember that you cannot change their circumstances or make things better for them; their grief is *their* journey to make. Be realistic in what you promise in terms of support and help. It is easy to get caught up in other people's emotional turmoil, and it is natural to want to do whatever is possible to help. However, promises made on the spur of the moment can sometimes be difficult to fulfil later on, so keep in mind what time and energy you have available.

People often remark about how much it helps to be able to talk openly about their grief to someone who understands. The ever-increasing pace and demands of everyday life leave little time and space for the bereaved person to gently work through the different aspects of their grief; pausing for a short while to allow another to feel support and care during their moment of need is a true kindness that we can extend to each other.

Resources

Books

A number of books have been published on different aspects of pet bereavement. The following are those I can personally recommend:

Garner, Angela. *Remembering My Pet*. UK: Environmental Animal Sanctuary and Education – EASE. This colourful activity book is designed to help children aged 11 years and under through the upset of losing a much-loved pet. It is free to download at https://ease-animals.org.uk

Hanh, Thich Nhat. *Fear: Essential Wisdom for Getting Through the Storm*. New York: HarperOne, 2012. The author explains how practical techniques of mindfulness can help us all, and shows how to ground ourselves in the present moment and find the courage to face what frightens us.

Ironside, Virginia. *Goodbye, Dear Friend: Coming to Terms with the Death of a Pet*. London, UK: JR Books, 2009. This book shares the experiences of others who have gone through a pet bereavement and brings solace and comfort.

Tuzeo-Jarolmen, JoAnn. *When a Family Pet Dies: A Guide to Dealing with Children's Loss.* London, UK: Jessica Kingsley Publishers, 2006. This concise book explains how children grieve at different ages, helping parents to understand how to talk to their children about the death of a family pet.

Websites

General

Child Bereavement UK. "Telling a Child that Someone Has Died." *https://www.childbereavementuk.org/telling-a-child-that-someone-has-died.*

Compassion Understood. *https://www.compassionunderstood.com/page/palliative-and-hospice-care-for-pets.* Palliative and hospice care for pets in the UK and US.

Environmental Animal Sanctuary & Education (EASE). Pet Loss Support. *https://ease-animals.org.uk/pet-loss-support/.* Pet loss bereavement support resources (audio and written).

International Association of Pet Cemeteries and Pet Crematories. *www.iaopc.com.*

The Rainbow Bridge. *https://en.wikipedia.org/wiki/Rainbow_Bridge _(pets).*

UK

Animal Trust. *https://www.animaltrust.org.uk/about-us.* North of England not-for-profit vets.

Association of Private Pet Cemeteries and Crematoria: *https://appcc.org.uk.*

Blue Cross. *https://www.bluecross.org.uk/pet-bereavement-and-pet-loss.* National pet bereavement support service.

"Fallen Stock and Safe Disposal of Dead Animals." UK Department for Environment, Food & Rural Affairs (DEFRA) and Animal and Plant Health Agency. 29 August 2012. Updated 11 May 2015. *https://www.gov.uk/guidance/fallen-stock.*

Lane, Martin. "How to Get Help with Vet Bills." *Money.co.uk.* 5 September 2018. *https://www.money.co.uk/pet-insurance/how-to -get-help-with-vet-bills.htm.*

The Maggie Fleming Animal Hospice. *https://www.themaggiefleminganimalhospice.org.uk.*

NHS: Help for Suicidal Thoughts. *https://www.nhs.uk/conditions /suicide/.* Suicide prevention helpline.

The Ralph Site. *https://www.theralphsite.com.* Pet bereavement resources and access to private counsellors.

The Samaritans. *https://www.samaritans.org.* Suicide prevention helpline.

"Six Places Pet Owners Can Go to Get Financial Help with Vet Bills." Vets Now. 10 September 2019. *https://www.vets-now.com/ 2018/02 /help-with-vet-bills.*

SupportLine. *https://www.supportline.org.uk/problems/pet-bereavement.* Confidential emotional support for pet bereavement.

US

American Foundation for Suicide Prevention. *https://afsp.org.*

Crisis Text Line. *https://www.crisistextline.org.*

Financial Assistance Information. *https://www.avma.org/resources /pet-owners/yourvet/financial-assistance-veterinary-care-costs.*

Green Pet Burial. *https://greenpetburial.org.* Promoting green pet burial sites.

Pet Loss Resources. Funeral Wise. *https://www.funeralwise.com/pet-loss /resources.*

Suicide Awareness Voices of Education (SAVE). *https://save.org.*

Suicide Prevention Lifeline. *https://suicidepreventionlifeline.org.*

United States National Suicide and Crisis Hotlines. *http://suicidehotlines.com/national.html.*

Australia & New Zealand

Beyond Blue. *https://www.beyondblue.org.au/get-support/get-immediate -support.* Suicide prevention, Australia.

Lifeline. *https://www.lifeline.org.au/get-help/get-help-home.* Suicide prevention, Australia.

Pet Medical Crisis. *https://petmedicalcrisis.com.au.* Financial assistance information, Australia.

Pets and People: Pet Loss and Grief Support and Counselling in Australia and New Zealand.
https://petsandpeople.com.au. Home page.
https://petsandpeople.com.au/pet-loss-counselling/new-zealands -first-pet-loss-support-hotline. New Zealand.

Services for Cat Owners. *https://www.cats.org.nz/services-for-cat-owners.* Services for cat owners in dire need in Canterbury, New Zealand, including financial assistance.

Suicide Prevention Australia. *https://www.suicidepreventionaust.org /contact-us.*

South Africa

LifeLine Johannesburg. *https://www.lifelinejhb.org.za/Suicide.ashx.* Mental health crisis (including suicidal thoughts).

South Africa Suicide Hotlines. *http://www.suicide.org/hotlines /international/south-africa-suicide-hotlines.html.*

The People's Dispensary for Sick Animals (PDSA). *https://www.pdsa.org. za/services.* Charitable support in pet care (tariff applies).

The South African Depression and Anxiety Group. *http://www.sadag.org /index.php?option=com_content&view=article&id=365:coping-with -loss-battling-bereavement-and-depression&catid=68&Itemid=132.* Help with anxiety and depression.

Acknowledgements

I am greatly indebted to the following individuals for their invaluable input into the production of this book:

Victoria M. Nicholls, BSc (Hons), BVetMed, Cert AVP (EM), Cert AVP (ED), BAEDT, MRCVS, who so kindly took the time to write the foreword for this book, and for sharing her moving poem about her dog, Frisby, as well as her amazing encouragement and support.

Anna Haines, BSc (Hons), MSc CAB, Full Member of The Association of Pet Behaviour Counsellors, Animal Behaviour & Training Council (ABTC), and Registered Clinical Animal Behaviourist, for her expertise on animal behaviour in the chapter on "Coping with Euthanasia for Pet Behaviour Problems".

Kevin Brown, BSc, PhD, BVMS, MRCVS, for his professional input in one of the activities.

Susan Smith-Wild, MASC (Relax), Professional Relaxation Therapist, for the relaxation and breathing exercises and for sharing her personal stories and experiences.

To the following for taking the time to read and give feedback on the various drafts: Eleanor Mestraud, BA (Hons) English & French (and for sharing her personal stories), Christine Gloag, and Chrissy Holmes.

To the following for their valued contributions: Melinda Hill for sharing her beautiful tribute to Mia, and for her incredible support for this book including professional proofreading of the final version; Hildreth Grace Rinehart, Director of Education and Equine Facilitator at Patch of Diamonds Ranch, for her moving story about Raja; Deirdre Chitwood, for sharing her thoughts on her beloved cat's end of life; Liz Ive, for sharing her personal thoughts and her poem; Lauren Jepson, for allowing me to include her childhood poem; the heartfelt contributions from my colleagues and friends at The Donkey Sanctuary: Heather Ross, Janneke Merkx, Claire Shapcott, Valentina Riva, Kate Pitts, Sara Whelan, and Amy Cripps; Rachel Dore, for her feedback on one of the activities; Ghislaine Silvers, for sharing her unique way of remembering her lovely greyhound, Nelson; and Mark Everitt, for kindly agreeing to share his personal story.

The Template Foundation, for its very special insights into the relationship between human and animal life.

My husband, Rob, and my close friends and family, for encouraging me in this quest.

NOTE: A number of the stories cannot be personally acknowledged, as they are taken from my experience of working with many people going through pet loss over the years. Whilst names and circumstances may have been changed to maintain confidentiality, there is no doubt that each and every person whom I have supported will have in some measure helped create this book. I am grateful to all who cared enough for their beloved pets that they grieved deeply for their losses.

About the Author

Photo by Chris Grady Photography

During 30 years in human healthcare as a Registered General Nurse, Angela Garner developed a strong interest in end-of-life issues and communicating in an empathic and sensitive way with the terminally ill, dying, and bereaved. Her life-long passion for animal welfare naturally led her to specialize in Companion Animal Bereavement Support.

Shortly after gaining her diploma in this area in 2001, she was asked to set up and run an innovative national pet bereavement support service for a small charity called Environmental Animal Sanctuary & Education (EASE), which now offers a full range of support resources created by the author.

Over the years, Angela has developed her own unique methods of communicating with bereaved pet owners and has written a wide range of support literature, including the Children's Pet Bereavement activity book on the EASE website. She has been awarded a fellowship by the Society of Bereavement Practitioners for her work. After learning to teach in the adult sector, she moved into training and lecturing on this subject.

In 2015, Angela was invited to lecture at the British Equine Veterinary Association (BEVA) annual conference, the video of which can be viewed on her website: **https://petlosspress.com.**

FINDHORN PRESS

Life-Changing Books

Learn more about us and our books at
www.findhornpress.com

For information on the Findhorn Foundation:
www.findhorn.org